SOCIAL SETTING, STIGMA,
AND COMMUNICATIVE COMPETENCE

Pragmatics & Beyond

An Interdisciplinary Series of Language Studies

VI:6

Sharon Sabsay, Martha Platt, et al.

Social Setting, Stigma, and Communicative Competence:
Explorations of the Conversational Interactions of Retarded Adults

SOCIAL SETTING, STIGMA, AND COMMUNICATIVE COMPETENCE:

Explorations of the Conversational Interactions of Retarded Adults

Sharon Sabsay, Martha Platt, *et al.*
University of California, Los Angeles

JOHN BENJAMINS PUBLISHING COMPANY
AMSTERDAM/PHILADELPHIA

1985

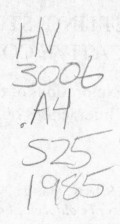

Library of Congress Cataloging in Publication Data

Sabsay, Sharon.
 Social setting, stigma, and communicative competence.

 (Pragmatics & beyond, ISSN 0166-6258; VI:6)
Bibliography: p.
1. Mentally handicapped -- United States. 2. Social interaction -- United States. 3. Inter-
personal communication -- United States. 4. Stigma (Social psychology) I. Platt, Martha.
II. Title. III. Series.
HV3006.A4S25   1985   362.3   86-8240
ISBN 90 272 2548 6 (European) / ISBN 0-915027-92-5 (US) (alk. paper)

TABLE OF CONTENTS

1. INTRODUCTION   1

   by Sharon Sabsay and Martha Platt

2. "ABOUT OSTRICHES COMING OUT OF COMMUNIST CHINA": MEANINGS, FUNCTIONS, AND FREQUENCIES OF TYPICAL INTERACTIONS IN GROUP MEETINGS FOR RETARDED ADULTS   9

   by Joseph Graffam

3. TAKING SIDES: RESOLUTION OF A PEER CONFLICT IN A WORKSHOP FOR RETARDED ADULTS   41

   by Kathryn M. Anderson-Levitt

4. DISPLAYING COMPETENCE: PEER INTERACTION IN A GROUP HOME FOR RETARDED ADULTS   75

   by Martha Platt

5. WEAVING THE CLOAK OF COMPETENCE: A PARADOX IN THE MANAGEMENT OF TROUBLE IN CONVERSATIONS BETWEEN RETARDED AND NONRETARDED INTERLOCUTORS   95

   by Sharon Sabsay and Martha Platt

FOOTNOTES   117

REFERENCES   121

APPENDIX A   125

APPENDIX B: Transcripts of episodes F, G, and L   129

1. INTRODUCTION

Sharon Sabsay and Martha Platt

Who are the retarded? Until recently, mentally retarded individuals, primarily children, have been studied almost exclusively as clinical entities. Their physical, intellectual, social, and linguistic limitations have been measured and described, but only rarely have they been treated as persons immersed in the stream of social life. Yet with changes in social policy in the last decade or so and federal legislation mandating that handicapped individuals be placed in the least restrictive environment commensurate with their needs and abilities, large numbers of individuals have been released from institutions and assisted in taking up life in the community. Many who had never been institutionalized are now receiving additional support and encouragement for independent living. Children currently being tested and identified as "developmentally disabled" are entitled to a broad range of services and provided with individual programs for education and training. When they reach school age, they are mainstreamed to the greatest extent possible. An entire industry has developed to provide services and training for the retarded after they leave school. Small board and care or group homes have been licensed, sheltered workshops established, vocational training programs developed, and vocational placement services provided. More than ever before, rather than being institutionalized or kept hidden in back bedrooms, retarded individuals are becoming a presence in the community.

In fact, so much a part of our lives have retarded individuals become that they have been the protagonists of an increasing number of novels such as *Sanjo*, nonfiction accounts such as *Like Normal People*, television and theatrical films such as *Bill* and *Best Boy*. While the public has had presented to it such images of the retarded, which convey a fuller picture of their lives and concerns, research has lagged behind. One notable exception has been the work of the Socio-Behavioral Research Group of the Mental Retardation Research Center at the University of California, Los Angeles. For almost ten years, members of this group have attempted to document, principally through ethnographic methods, the lives of mildly retarded adults living in the community — at home with parents or siblings, in large board and care facilities and smaller group homes, with roommates, lovers, or spouses. Studies have investigated such areas as work, use of leisure time, the nature of social support networks, adolescence, socio-emotional adjustment, and communicative competence.

What is mental retardation? According to the definition accepted by the American Association on Mental Deficiency, "mental retardation refers to subnormal general intellectual functioning which originates during the developmental period and is associated with impairment in adaptive behavior" (Heber 1961: 499). Subnormal intellectual functioning is defined as performance on measures of general intelligence (i.e., IQ tests) more than two standard deviations below the population mean (100) of the age group involved. Usually this means an IQ score of seventy or below, although states and social agencies may establish different criteria. Adaptive behavior is defined as the effectiveness of the individual in adapting to the natural and social demands of his environment. It is usually measured in terms of social, emotional, and personal adjustment. (See, for example, Meyers, Nihira, and Zetlin 1979). In actual practice, however, mental retardation tends to get treated as a unidimensional phenomenon related primarily to intellectual functioning, and IQ scores remain the principal measure of retardation (e.g., Mercer 1973; Langness 1976).

Although mental retardation is usually thought of as a condition based on some organic disorder, 85% of the people in the United States classified as retarded are "functionally" retarded. Functionally retarded individuals are those who are mildly retarded (i.e., those with IQ scores between 55 and 70) and have no evident organic disorder or brain pathology. Organically retarded individuals, those who have physiological defects and tend to have IQ's lower than 50, constitute the other 15% of the estimated six million plus retarded individuals in the United States. The individuals who are the subjects of these studies fall into the mildly and moderately retarded range and are for the most part functionally retarded.

Language and mental retardation. The literature on the language of the mentally retarded suggests that difficulties with language and communication constitute one of the major problem areas for the retarded individual. In fact, linguistic deficits are almost a defining feature of mental retardation. Until recently, studies of the language of individuals with retardation have focused almost exclusively on linguistic competence, documenting the extent of deficits in articulation, syntax, morphology, and vocabulary. In the past few years there has been an increasing realization of the need to investigate language use as well as language structure. Despite a number of programmatic calls, however, little research has been done in this area. Moreover, there has been a recognition of the need to pay attention to the contexts in which language is used by retarded individuals and the communicative demands of those situations, but the settings in which language competence is evaluated continue to be for the most part relatively unnatural ones, and the range of skills investigated limited. We know little of the ability of retarded individuals to manage the give and take of everyday conversation, to gain and hold the floor, to explain and resolve problems, to handle a variety of instrumental and social interactions. The full range of settings in which retarded individuals actually use language have not been identified, nor have the characteristics of those settings and the extent of their influence on verbal behavior been recognized. Unless the characteristics of the settings and the concerns of these who operate within them are understood, however, the functional nature of the talk which occurs is likely to be missed and may lead to the underestimation or misperception of retarded speakers' verbal competence. As the papers in this volume show, verbal behavior which at first glance appears to be aberrant or deficient, can, if analyzed with reference to the context, interactional history, and social concerns, be seen to be functional for the participants, and at times even highly skilled.

Setting, stigma, and communicative competence. The papers in this volume are all concerned with how the conversational interactions in which mentally retarded speakers participate are affected by their communicative and intellectual incompetence, by their stigmatized identity, and by the social setting in which such interactions take place. The social interactions examined are typical of those in which mentally retarded adults engage on a day to day basis with both retarded and nonretarded interlocutors. A critical characteristic of the contexts in which these interactions take place is that they are in some way shaped by recognition of the incompetence of the retarded participants, be it their inability to live independently, to find competitive employment, or to manage their everyday affairs without the intervention of a more competent person. Perhaps the most basic issue addressed in these investigations is the concern of retarded and nonretarded interlocutors alike with the social stigma associated with intellectual incompetence. This concern is seen to underlie patterns of verbal behavior, attitudes, and values of retarded speakers, and the nature of accommodations made by nonretarded speakers to the often poorly organized discourse and inappropriate conversational behavior of their retarded interlocutors. The insights provided by these studies are only made possible by analysis of recordings and transcripts of spontaneous talk in natural settings, informed by detailed ethnographic observations.

Each paper in this volume explores two aspects of the contexts in which interactions occur, the setting and the participants, and attempts to show the contribution each makes to the nature of talk. The particular features of the conversational settings that are seen to be important for the purposes of these investigations are the roles that they establish for the participants and the institutional goals that operate within them. The particular features of participants that are important are the individual definitions and understandings that they bring to the interactions apart from their roles, and their private concerns and agendas. These two major aspects of context together are seen as crucial determinants of the nature and outcome of a particular conversational interaction.

All of the papers are concerned in varying degrees with three major aspects of verbal interaction. The first is the moment-to-moment mechanics of conversational interaction, such as gaining the floor, accomplishing speaker change, and introducing topics. The second is the management of information, both what is talked about and how it is presented. The third, and perhaps most important, is the strategies used by participants to accomplish interactional goals and the particular nature of those goals for these individuals.

Graffam's paper serves as an introduction to this population in the setting of a sheltered workshop. It focuses on weekly group discussion sessions among some of the Workshop's retarded employees or "clients." These discussion sessions, while an ongoing part of the participants' daily routine, nonetheless involve a suspension of the interactional constraints of the larger setting. During the weekly meetings, topics or behaviors discouraged by the Workshop authorities can be freely engaged in. In this arena, as Graffam argues, participants have been able to evolve a set of rules and practices related to language use that clearly reflect their concerns and the nature of this particular conversational context as "time out" from the stigma of their intellectual incompetence.

Anderson-Levitt's paper builds on Graffam's by focusing on the way in which participants in the group meeting discuss and resolve conflicts with peers in the Workshop. She demonstrates that the talk occurring in such interactions, which appears at first incompetent and incoherent, is, if the shared culture and history of the Workshop clients is taken into account, actually strategic and effective. Anderson-Levitt shows that the verbal strategies speakers use (the types of arguments they raise, etc.) are intimately linked to the commonly held values and concerns of the group members and that this relationship ultimately shapes both the course and outcome of such discussions.

By contrast, Platt describes the verbal interaction of residents of a small board and care facility, or "group home." Just as interaction in the group meeting is a reflection of participants' common goals and aspirations and the character of that setting as "time out" from normal constraints, conversation in the group home is also a reflection of the participants' concerns and the character of the setting. Rather than providing a respite from stigmatized status, however, the group home is a setting which by its very nature emphasizes residents' inability to perform competently in the outside world and thus implicitly accentuates their "less-than-adult" status. Established routines and practices in the group home, organized to facilitate acquisition and practice of everyday skills, create a context in which conversational interaction centers on displays of mundane knowledge. These displays generate aberrant conversations, but they are in fact a functional response to a context which places a priority on evidencing competence. Similar displays are common in the group meetings, reflecting the fact that members of the group meetings and residents the group home share many of the same goals and concerns. But in the group meetings these goals are jointly pursued, whereas in the group home they are pursued individually. This is reflected in the fact that interactions in the group home have a confrontational nature, involving challenges of such displays and demands for objective proof or demonstration, while claims of competence in the group meetings are supported and elaborated on by co-participants, sometimes in total disregard of objective truth.

Virtually every social interaction in which retarded individuals participate is to some degree influenced by the fundamental reality of the stigma attached to intellectual and social incompetence. Even in the Workshop and group home, where they are somewhat sheltered from society at large and interact primarily with their peers, retarded individuals manifest a constant concern with self-presentation and the denial or masking of incompetence. However, as Sabsay and Platt argue, it is in interaction with nonretarded interlocutors that disguising or concealing incompetence becomes an overriding concern for all participants. Their paper explores some of the problems that the intellectual and social deficits of mildly retarded speakers create for others in conversation and the ways in which concern for these persons' self-esteem influences how the resulting communicative and interactional trouble is managed. This investigation also reveals, however, that efforts to repair interaction may also have the effect of creating more trouble by drawing attention to incompetence and thereby damaging the self-esteem of the retarded individual.

For social scientists who already recognize the importance of understanding the social context in which language is used, the special nature of the interactional contexts and the participants explored in this volume should provide new insights into the effects of stigmatized social identity on the nature and structure of talk. These papers should also be of interest to those who study the accommodations conversational participants must make to conversationally less competent interlocutors such as children and foreigners. Finally, although mentally retarded speakers are members of the broader speech community and both share and are judged in terms of that community's traditions, norms, and values for language use, they have also developed a unique set of patterns of verbal behavior, attitudes, practices, and concerns which are derived from their identity as stigmatized persons. Thus they might be said to be members of a more restricted speech community of a rather unusual character, and studies of their language use should provide new insights into the development and organization of speech communities and the origins of norms and values of language use.

For those interested in the mentally retarded for personal or professional reasons, this volume offers a perspective and richness of insight rarely found in studies of language and mental retardation. By portraying the verbal behavior of retarded individuals as in large part a response to features of the social environment, rather than simply as a consequence of their intellectual handicap, these studies show mildly and moderately retarded adults to be active and skillful interlocuters, using their understanding of various social situations to formulate their contributions to conversational interaction.

The studies on which these papers are based are part of ongoing ethnographic research conducted by the Socio-Behavioral Group of the Mental Retardation Research Center at the University of California at Los Angeles. The studies by Graffam, Anderson-Levitt, and Platt were conducted while the authors were United States Public Health Service Pre- and Post-Doctoral National Institute of Child Health and Human Development Trainees with the Socio-Behavioral Group (National Research Service Award No. 07032). Research on all four papers was supported by NICHD Program Project Grant HD 11944-04 and National Institute of Education Grant NIE-G-80-0016. Research at the Workshop was part of the ongoing Workshop Society Project, directed by Jim Turner. The names used in all four papers for study participants are pseudonyms.

2. "ABOUT OSTRICHES COMING OUT OF COMMUNIST CHINA": MEANINGS, FUNCTIONS, AND FREQUENCIES OF TYPICAL INTERACTIONS IN GROUP MEETINGS FOR RETARDED ADULTS

Joseph Graffam

2.1 Introduction

It is March 9, 1977 at 2 p.m. Inside a small conference room at a "sheltered workshop", a group of moderately and mildly mentally retarded clients have begun to assemble for one of the over 600 "group meetings" that have been held there between 1975 and 1982. Stan shouts, "Where's the rest of the nation? Where's Mr. Moloney [a fellow client], 'The Pride of the Nation'? Where's the rest of the nation?" (He is referring to the tardiness of certain group members.) Stan then complains about a client who has been suspended from the workshop for breaking some cardboard containers. Dale interrupts, "I don't want to hear another 'broken record'!" He then repeats what Stan has already said. The group talks about Don Snitch, the suspended client, bringing up his behavior problems and his current marital status (as one of only a few married clients). A few more clients enter the room and one asks, "Where's Jim [Turner]?" The group discusses the possible whereabouts of the psychologist-researcher from UCLA; one member suggests locking him out of the room (which is momentarily done) and the group laughs. As Turner enters the meeting, Penny begins to describe her birthday party and names some of the gifts she received. Two members report problems they are having at home: one man has a grandfather sick with "sunstroke," and a woman has been punched in the eye by a relative and is sporting a black eye at present. Penny cuts short this woman's statement in order to report having taken a weekend trip to the San Diego Zoo and having seen Yvette driving around over the weekend. Yvette adds that a friend of hers has just bought a new "bus" and he likes to "drive around and tell jokes." "Dirty jokes?", asks Turner. Stan takes the digression further by asking, "Dirty jokes? About ostriches coming out of communist China?" Turner then queries, "Is there a joke about that?", to which Stan replies, "No, that's no joke!" Discussion continues for another 45 minutes. (For a more complete, actual transcript, see Appendix A.)

This vignette serves as an introduction by immersion into the unique and complex interaction setting of group meetings for mild and moderately mentally retarded adults. As in all such interactions, much that takes place within the group meetings is informed by and based on a wider context. Thus, informed by relevant background information about the group and its members, one may hope to get the joke about the ostriches, and the meaning of much else that takes place in these meetings. First, a brief history of the relationship between Dr. Jim Turner (and his associates) and the administration, staff, and clients at New Horizons Workshop is in order. Originally, Turner, a research professor at UCLA, approached the administrators at New Horizons offering to run a group meeting at the workshop in exchange for the opportunity to carry on ethnographic research within the workshop setting (Turner 1983). Members of the counseling staff assigned a number of the more aggressive male clients to Turner's "violence group," as it was initially termed. The first recorded meeting was held on 11/5/75. Over the course of the next seven+ years, over 90 clients have participated in the meetings on a more or less regular basis. Generally, between eight and twelve clients have been members at any given time of one of the two or three groups which have operated continuously. Following the initial assignments, most clients have become group members on the basis of self-selection. An informal waiting list of hopeful candidates has existed for some time as well. The drop-out rate is low, however, and a large number of prospective members wait indefinitely.

There are few rules for group participation. Members may talk about any topic, event, or situation they choose, but the confidence of the group is to be protected. No one is allowed to divulge group proceedings to nonmembers. Individuals have at times been accused of such a breach and been subject to reprimands from fellow group-members. Individual members have likewise been prevented by their peers from discussing certain subjects from time to time (e.g., death, sex, handicap). Such exceptions appear to be situationally determined, and in general confidentiality and free speech *have* been honored. To date, over 620 hours of audiotaped group meetings have been conducted, providing insight into ethnographic questions relevant to the workshop as a whole and emerging as a rich source of data in themselves. With such a large number (90+) of individuals involved and given the longitudinal nature of the research, an analysis of the content of group discussions can provide fairly accurate insight into the nature and consistency or change of focal concerns of the workshop client population in general. Likewise, an analysis of group process with respect to socio-emotional need/ satisfaction can provide insight into the process of socio-emotional adjustments among workshop clients. Moreover, given the large number of individuals involved and the large total number of sessions conducted over such a prolonged period of time, the results of any such analyses can be seen as extremely relevant to a more general discussion of counseling or therapy for retarded persons.

The purpose of the study reported here was to order the data contained in the body of group meeting tapes in a manner which on one hand explains the phenomenon of the groups as a whole, and on the other provides a set of relevant facts or characteristics of the group meeting phenomenon which accommodates analysis and understanding of particular events or event sequences. The procedure for selecting tapes from the total inventory for inclusion in this sample was very straightforward. Starting with the tape of the first meeting, 11/5/75, one tape was selected from each month, alternating between Group #1 and Group #2 whenever possible.[1] If there were no existent tapes for one or more consecutive months, the next taped session available was included. Tape selection varied from early to middle to late in the months so as to obtain a relatively equal distribution from day 1 to day 31. A total of 77 tapes were included in the sample, which concludes with the end of 1982 (12/22/82). After 25 tapes were listened to and rough transcriptions were made, a set of categories of topics was generated (see Table 1). It was then possible to chart frequency distributions for each category (and in many cases subcategories) with a minimun of residual topics for all 77 meetings. Notes were taken on the specific topics so finer distinctions could be made later within categories. Notes were also taken on various salient aspects of group dynamics (e.g., status of speaker, turntaking, group responsiveness and reactivity). Although strict tabulation was not carried out, the relative frequencies of prominent interaction styles or modes were noted in the listing of incidents. In short, an attempt has been made to provide at least rough quantification of the *content* and *dynamics* of group meetings. In some instances, judgments were made about topic changes, shifts in who held "the floor," and so forth, so the accuracy of any frequency count is open to some speculation. However, the potential for significant error has been reduced by the large sample of tapes reviewed and almost three years of attendance at these group meetings prior to this endeavor. (In retrospect, such familiarity seems an essential to the task.)

Rather than simply presenting the accumulated figures and the notes which relate to those figures in the manner of some teletype, presentation of the data seems best handled via reimmersion. On the basis of information extracted from the sample of tapes one could probably construct a synthetic, reasonably accurate facsimile of a hypothetical group meeting. However, a more efficient and perhaps more exact rendering of the data is accomplished by applying to the initial introductory vignette an element-by-element analysis of the contextual meanings, relative frequencies, and functional properties of such types of interactions within the group meetings as a whole. For this purpose, a more complete, though not exhaustive, transcript will be employed (see Appendix A), one which extends further into the meeting than the vignette. Any important features of the group meetings which do not emerge from this analysis will be discussed when they become relevant to particular points of discussion.

2.2. Example 1

Again, it is March 9, 1977 at 2 p.m. In the conference room, clients have begun to gather for the scheduled meeting. From the cacophony of voices comes one a bit louder and more exuberant:

Stan: Where's the rest of the nation? ((repeated 3 times)) We rode our bikes to work today. I gotta steer Ken's [his brother] home. He left it here.

Brad: I gotta go to work. Gil needs me to stack boxes.

Deac: Tell him [Jim Turner] your problems then get out.

2.2.1. Introductions

Stan's eagerness to begin the meetings seems to border on impatience. His initial, repeated question about tardy members is an indirect attempt to start proceedings and communicates two of the basic characteristics of the group meeting phenomenon as a whole, informality and negotiation. More often, meetings are begun with direct and obvious introductory statements. Metaphors are commonly employed for initiating action and conveying informality. At various times clients have announced, "Action! Roll 'em!," "Order in the Court!," "Quiet on the set!," or some other figurative request or demand for action. One man has come to regard himself as a Master of Ceremonies of sorts, opening each meeting by announcing into the microphone, "Ladies and Gentlemen, this is Jim Turner's group (then introducing each member present along with researchers by name). And now, Ladies

Table 1. Frequency of topics discussed in group meetings

Categories of Topics Discussed	Frequency in Sample (of 77)	
Dreams	40 reported in	21 meetings
Eventfulness Reports	81	44
Practical Problems	30	22
Personal Problems (at shop)	167	58
peers	137	58
staff	20	16
self	10	7
Other People's Problems	74	37
Competency Claims	57	49
normalcy fabrications	6	6
grandiose claims/alter identity	6	6
competency displays (actual)	45	28
Problems at home	76	37
sick relatives	29	21
familial conflict	26	25
teasing/abuse	11	8
overrestrictiveness	10	6
Events in Others' Lives	24	19
Issues of World-view (Societal norms and values)	33	28
Researcher Initiated Questions	11	11

and Gentlemen, Jim Turner." Metaphors from the entertainment world predominate. In the case of the meeting cited above, Stan's rhetorical question was an allusion to "Face the Nation," at the time one of his oft-mentioned shows. On occasion, of course, clients have become somewhat impatient with such a slow process and simply taken direct steps to get things going by ordering, "Okay! Be quiet! Now let's go. I got lots to talk about today." Even with such abrupt commands, some measure of humor usually sustains the informal atmosphere in which the meetings have come to thrive.

2.2.2. *Practical problems*

Stan *does* begin the meeting, with a seemingly nondescript statement about having ridden bikes to work. Once he adds a qualifying statement (almost three minutes later) to the effect that his brother has gone on a trip for the day and has left his bicycle behind, it is more apparent that Stan has presented a practical problem to the group. Such problems are not the most commonly reported type of problem in group meetings; only 29 such reports of practical problems were made in the 77 meetings sampled. Most of those reports pertained to the need for money, problems with medications, problems with Medi-Cal or a social worker, lost lunches or articles of clothing, and a recurring problem of broken toilets due to soft drink cans or screws being flushed down. This last problem was unique in that it affected more than just one client and was more than simply a practical problem. Complaints about the loss of privacy, dignity, and adult status generally accompanied the reports of broken toilets, since restrooms were patrolled and doors were removed from stalls following such incidents. In general, however, reports of practical problems were noncontroversial and personal. Seldom did advice follow such reports. Stan's reported problem is representative of this type of problem in these respects.

2.2.3. *The purpose of the meetings*

Continuing with the above transcript: Brad's statement implies that in his opinion the meeting has *not* started yet, but that he will have to leave soon nevertheless. Deac offers a solution, "Tell him your problems, then get out." Indeed, airing one's "problems" is one of the purposes clients identify for the meetings. In the initial meeting, Turner asked the then-members what they would like to do or discuss in the meetings. The group was at first divided between "the shop" and "whatever we want." It is obvious that the faction taking the more general view has held sway as membership has changed and time has passed. In the 77 meetings sampled, the topic of why the meetings exist was brought up six times, twice by the researcher and four times by clients, usually in response to a new member's having joined the group in question. On such occasions, clients not only explain the purposes of the group but explain rules of confidentiality, etc. Individual explanations of group purpose include "to talk about our feelings," "to talk about problems," "to get things off your chest." Likewise, other clients have held to the more general position, "It's an open-minded meeting, we can talk about anything we want!" In fact, as will come out, much of group discussion has little or nothing to do with problems per se. However, in the sample of meetings, when a client explanation of the purpose of group meetings was specific, *problems and their resolution* predominated as an explanation of why the group meetings exist.[2]

2.3. Example 2

Stan:	Don Snitch broke those containers. Yesterday. ((group laughter))
Deac:	I heard about it. ((repeated three times)) I don't need a broken record. Don Snitch broke some containers yesterday.
Stan:	He got suspended.
Edie:	His wife was crying too.
Deac:	Sure she was!
Edie:	I feel sorry for her.

2.3.1. *Labeling*

Deac's claim that Stan sounds like a "broken record" is one common in the wider social context of the workshop and not unheard of within group meetings. Within the workshop, *labels* are primarily reserved for those clients who chronically and consistently violate implicit behavior norms of the client population. Individuals who persist in reporting personal problems with staff or peers, those who precipitate such problems, those who make threats of physical violence, or even those who persist in verbal aggression are likely to be added to the list of recognized workshop "troublemakers." Those given to highly emotional reactions such as extreme jubilation (jumping and clapping hands) or easy and deep remorse (sobbing too readily too often), those who suck their thumbs, those who have "temper tantrums" are likely to be labeled "babies." "Crazy" or "maniac" are terms usually reserved for those who either engage in uncontrolled fantasies or are extremely aggressive. Such ascriptions are less common and in many cases are applied as descriptive terms rather than as enduring labels. Don Snitch, the client dicussed during this meeting, was one named repeatedly in various meetings and for various reasons as "crazy." "Tattletale" describes not only those who report misbehaviors to authority personnel, but those who spread "rumors" and break confidences as well. So, within the workshop certain labels are used to describe particularly bothersome or deviant individuals and within the group meetings certain workshop clients are accused of behavior in consonance with the labels. In the 77 meetings sampled, a label was ascribed to a nonmember in 58 meetings; in most cases a number of reports were made of unspecified bad behavior (e.g., "He was bothering me too!"). The actual number of workshop clients accused of behavior worthy of label ascriptions was only eight in this sample, but lists obtained independently from individuals naming such clients were considerably longer, with a fair amount of overlap. At any rate, in the example in the transcript, Deac has accused Stan, a fellow group member, of being a "broken record." In the entire sample Stan was accused two additional times of sounding "just like a broken record." Kit likewise was described as "a broken record, going around and around." Deanne added, "They're calling them repeaters. They make me nauseous." In fact, Stan in this instance may have reported "old news," but he had not repeated it over and over at that point. Deac is either making reference to Stan's having fixated constantly on this event for the past day or is anticipating Stan's getting repetitive later in the group meeting. Either or both are probable explanations and consistent with Stan's somewhat idiosyncratic style of interaction. Ascribing labels to group members, with the exception of the "broken record" label, is apparently in bad taste, as group members have been accused of proscribed bad behavior (in the sample) but avoided having labels ascribed. Of course, not all deviant behavior is labeled and the fact that some behavior escapes labeling does not indicate that all labeling is in bad taste.

2.3.2. The personalization of problems

Another element in this piece of transcript is the discussion of what might at first glance be termed *other people's problems*: Don broke some containers, was suspended, and his wife is upset about it. Problems in other clients' lives were reported 74 times in 37 of the meetings sampled. Most common were others' problems with affiliative relationships at the workshop (who broke up with whom, fights between friends, etc.). Other people's problems at home (parental or sibling divorce, sick relative, domestic arguments, disciplining of the client, etc.) were also commonly reported. Frequent mention was made of other clients being "bugged" by some unnamed "troublemaker."

This marked concern with other people's problems is related to one of the focal concerns of the client population in general, that is, the maintenance of social harmony (Turner 1983). In addition to deep and pervasive concern with the maintenance of social harmony, another characteristic of the workshop population in general and the group meetings in particular that partially explains the attention and involvement in others' problems is that of an *emotionality contagion*. (It remains unclear, however, whether a contagiousness of emotionality leads to involvement in others' problems or whether involvement in others' problems leads to shared emotions.) At any rate, a highly emotional response to some problem, usually one's own, followed by equally or more intense reactions by fellow group-members, is a relatively common in-group phenomenon. On numerous occasions discussion of certain subjects (death, dead parents, or even Elvis Presley, for example) has led to first one member, then another, and then others bursting into tears over some personal, private conflict. The reporting of certain events (a favorite supervisor leaving the "shop," the death of a fellow client, or, on the reverse side, a staff member getting married or having a baby) has likewise within numerous meetings led to a highly charged reaction which has spread through at least a portion of the group. The intensity of these "contagious" emotional reactions varies according to both the severity of the problem reported and the relative status of the group member reporting or first reacting (a more or less popular or valued member). Often, reported incidents are much less dramatic than the examples given, though reactions may be equally as contagious. In many cases such responses appear to be akin to "sympathy pains" of some sort. In the transcript, Edie's statement of sympathy might be seen in that light, although usually responses are more pronounced and more communal.

2.4. Example 3

Stan:	Did he break up his marriage?
Deac:	No! Not yet! ((many voices echo Deac's denial with gusto))
Stan:	He's going to!
Deac:	No he isn't. ((the rest agree heartily)) He's not going to!
Rick:	No. He gonna take this ring forever.
Deac:	That's true. ((several again agree heartily))

2.4.1. *On societal norms and values*

Edie has reported that Don's wife is upset about his suspension. Stan then asks the group how severe the personal aspect of the problem is ("Did he break up his marriage?"). The group responds adamantly and univocally with a denial that includes an affirmation of the permanence of marriage. An initial point worth making is that while at any given time in the period from 1975 to 1982 marriages within the workshop client population have been extremely rare, marriage remains a fundamental feature of many clients' future plans. The success of existing marriages may be viewed by clients as a reflection of their own future prospects for marriage. The belief that "marriage is forever" has been repeated again and again within group meeting discussions and is consonant with the general tenor of the ethics expressed by participants.

Discussions of societal norms, beliefs, and values took place 33 times in 28 of the meetings sampled. Religion, politics, and marriage predominated as topics. Religious discussions covered the existence or nonexistence of God, Hell, and the Devil, grace vs. good works, death and afterlife, doctrinal differences, and religions of the world. Political discussions included the topics of race relations, law and order, the degeneracy of contemporary society, the history of Man, freedom of choice, Nazism, and several discussions on the relative merits of the "circus animals" (Republican elephants) and the "stubborn ol' mules" (Democrats). Discussions of marriage and married life ranged from talk about the lives of normal adults to the particular do's and don'ts of weddings, how people work, play, pay bills, etc.

These discussions of the societal norms, beliefs, and values consistently display a conservative, neo-Victorian, perhaps Puritanical ideology. With few exceptions, discussants showed themselves to be rather staunch traditionalists, both morally and politically. Discussions of alcohol and drug use have likewise demonstrated this conservatism. However, in other contexts the very same clients who have vehemently opposed the use of alcohol have admitted liking or wanting to drink beer.

2.4.2. Consensus-seeking

Another facet of the group experience revealed in this part of the transcript is seeking and gaining (hopefully) a consensus among one's peers. In this case Stan seems to ask a rather straightforward question ("Did he break up his marriage?"). Deac responds firmly in the negative, then qualifies ("Not yet!"). He then gets obvious backing from the group. Stan is *not* a highly regarded group member, but one who would probably have difficulty gaining a consensus on "God is nice." This points up the fact that the relative status of members is a factor in the gaining of a consensus, as much as is the nature and position held in an argument. In this case Deac is defending a moral (and morally conservative rather than progressive) position popular among his peers and gaining a consensus is thus made easier. Rick joins the discussion ("He gonna take this ring forever.") and Deac agrees, followed by several other members.

Rather than waiting for support, one might also actively solicit the opinion(s) of other highly regarded, influential, and predictably agreeable group members. On occasion, certain clients have done so either prior to or following the disclosure of their own position. For example, in response to a problem his girlfriend was having at home Jack volunteered, "I think you should do what your mother says. What do you think Phil?" On another occasion, regarding a potentially more controversial argument, Jack offered, "Hmmm, what do you think about that Phil?", then agreed with the other's statement. In the meeting under examination, though further along, a number of clients are heard to say, "I agree about that," in response to comments they themselves have just made, as if agreeing with oneself can somehow strengthen one's argument. Focussing attention on a recognized workshop "troublemaker," or someone who is "crazy" or a "baby" makes it considerably easier to gain a consensus than would attacking a popular client or a member of the group itself. If one is able to read the situation at hand and adeptly employ persons and positions popular within the group, even a relatively low-status member of the group might gain a consensus. Certain individuals, though very few in number, have at various times been able to sustain an argument without gaining or succumbing to a consensus, because of eloquence, aggressiveness, or impenetrable stubbornness. These instances, however, are considerably less common.

2.5. Example 4

Deac: He's mean and nasty, he swears.
Group: I know!
Deac: She's not here because Don's not here.
Rick: Well what happened? She get suspended?
Deac: No, Don did so she stayed home.
Rick: Don got suspended, ha! That's his fault. You never swear in the workshop.
Deac: Yes, he does. He says goddamnit and all that stuff. He does.
Edie: Hey! Watch your mind kid!
Stan: Hallelujah!
Deac: No, he don't say hallelujah. ((much laughter))

2.5.1. Personal problems with peers

Deac has implied that the problem with Don Snitch is more than simply work-related and involves more than his private life. (Stan may have meant the same thing from the start.) Don is "mean and nasty," a problem for those around him, indeed a problem for clients as a whole. Problems within the workshop were reported 167 times in 58 of the 77 meetings sampled. Twenty of these involved staff members who were "too bossy," "mean," called clients names, monitored behavior too closely, and the like. Ten were reported as being due to the speaker's own inabilities or personality characteristics, and did not involve other persons. In the remaining 137 instances in which the topic of personal problems at the workshop was raised, the subject was *problems with peers*. In these instances, most often more than one member reported having had a similar problem with the same person to whom blame had been attributed by the preceding speaker. Approximately half of all such reports were of unspecified or generally stated problems with one of the recognized workshop deviants. Such persons were accused of "bugging" or "bothering" either the speaker or someone with whom the speaker associates, either "on the bus," "on my line," or during break or lunch time. In the case cited here, Don has been accused of being "mean and nasty," rather a general complaint, but also of "swearing," Rick adding that, "You never swear in the workshop!" A great many of the peer-problems reported in the sample of meetings had to do with the violation of implicit workshop client norms of behavior.

2.5.2. *Workshop social rules*[3]

The most commonly reported complaint of rule violation had to do with the *spreading of rumors*, an offense potentially attributable to any client, named or nameless. "Rumors" are said to turn people against one another, cause fights, stir up trouble. "Talking behind my back" and various permutations of that offense have been repeatedly brought up. "It's like snooping and repeating. That's bad!" Such rumors are generally treated as false, but the question of subversiveness is more important than that of falsehood, which is less often and less emphatically stated. Almost as common were reported *threats or acts of physical violence*. Such behavior is obviously against the rules of both clients and administration, yet is regularly reported. Many of the complaints are probably more imagined than real, the result perhaps of exaggeration and a little misunderstanding at times. Sue reported more than once, "Martin is threatening me with a knife, he wants to rape me!" Many incidents are of the "almost" variety: "She almost hit me in my surgery," "Pat threw some trash in the wastebasket and almost hit Anne!", etc. In the entire sample there were three reported acts of physical violence: one slap in the face, one bloody nose, and one biting incident. Most of the complaints of peer-initiated threats were actually accounts of shouting matches or rather obvious posturing. Earlier in the history of the group meetings, some of these threats and gestures were made within the group and involved members only. Such behavior became much less prevalent as membership changed over time.

No teasing or namecalling is also a frequently invoked rule and violations of this rule are frequently reported. Teasing and namecalling include the use of labels employed to mark recognized chronic offenders, and any reference to a person's handicap or any other term implying intellectual inferiority ("Stupid," "Dummy," "Retarded").

Sex offenses of sorts are the next most frequently reported type of rule violation in the sample. The implicit rule violated in these cases is *no sex at the workshop*, a rule invoked when convenient. A number of men have been accused of "kissing boys" and engaging in other homosexual activities either in the men's bathroom or outside the building. A number of reported "petting" incidents have occurred as well (men with volunteers and draftees alike). A few men have been accused of looking either up or down women's blouses. "Going behind the workshop" is the euphemistic way of referring to perhaps more advanced stages of "hanky panky."

Complaints of clients *acting "bossy"* were relatively common in the sample as well. Almost every complaint of bossiness had to do with job performance per se. Reports of persons *staring at or following other clients* are likewise frequently reported in the sample. Such alleged incidents are seen and sometimes described as violations or invasions of privacy, but often appear to be little more than attempts to join a smaller group of friends: for example, Roger complained, "Deac just follows us around like a puppy dog." Anne's complaint about Emma was obviously due to Emma's overzealous ambitions for friendship: "Emma was staring at Pat and me at lunch. She does it all the time." (Long term observations outside of the group substantiate the author's conclusion.) In the transcript, Deac accuses Don of *swearing*; this too is a relatively common complaint made in the meetings sampled. When evidence is offered, almost any word(s) can suffice, from "shut up," "shit," and "damnit," up to the more complex descriptive terms. Gestures are also referred to periodically (the workshop "finger" is the index finger for those interested).

Finally, *tattletaling* is a frequent complaint. There were two accusations of a group member having "blabbed" some secrets outside of the group meeting and broken confidentiality. Most reports were of other clients having told staff members of the speaker's minor infractions on the line or in the yard. One man confessed having reported a "humping" incident to staff, then said he "told" himself. He added, "It's okay to tell a supervisor, but not a counselor. There's a rule against tattletaling." This statement in many ways tells it all, in that the speaker himself brings up the rule against tattletaling having just admitted having done it. Such is the case with many clients and many of the group members with regard to many of these informal rules. One may vehemently condemn someone for a single, minor infraction when the accuser is a chronic offender in that area. (Much like the rest of us, these people understand that a "good person" is one who knows the rules and isn't afraid to say so.) Outside of these meetings, the bulk of members and non-members are by no means compliant, but are very much concerned with compliance in general.

2.6. Example 5

Two members of the group, routinely tardy due to special work schedules, now arrive at the conference room. Jim Turner has yet to enter:

Roger: Hey! Now we're early and he's late today!

Deac: He came in, plugged it [taperecorder] in and left.

Stan: Hold it! Where's the nation? Where's the rest of our nation? The whole nation must be here!

Deac: Jim walked out the door before Roger and Rudy got here.

Roger: Lock the door! ((someone does this and much laughter follows))

Deac: No, don't do that! Lonnie, unlock that door! Don't lock the door.

Stan: Where's the rest of the nation?

((Jim Turner now enters the room))

Dean: There's Jim. You're late!

Stan: The whole nation must be here!

2.6.1. *An arena of normalcy*

For members of the various groups, involvement provides welcome relief (perhaps even reprieve) from a primarily regulated, monitored, and dependent existence. The informality of the group meeting context is exemplified again in this bit of the transcript where late-arrivals enter, ask Turner's whereabouts, lock him out, laugh about this, and then accuse him of being late when he does enter. Status distinctions to which clients have become accustomed are temporarily relaxed, and although Turner and other researchers may be vested with authority, the style, indeed technique, is non-directive, and there is no teacher-student or counselor-client relationship per se. The fact that meetings are run not by individuals who are a part of the workshop authority structure, but by "outsiders," no doubt encourages informality and increased self-disclosure. A sense of a group-ness has evolved. In the earlier meetings sampled, members tended to address Turner directly and to follow preceding speakers with seemingly unrelated "private agenda" reports of their own interest. Through time, more people have more often addressed the group in general and remained more on topic than they did earlier.

Behavior within the group meetings is unregulated for the most part. In the entire sample there was only a single instance of Turner having intervened by denying the speaker right to continue (the speaker had threatened to "kill" a fellow client). Members are free to express virtually any emotion, to use "spicy" language, to berate superiors or parents and care providers, to fantasize. Yelling, crying, and other displays of extreme emotion are generally frowned upon outside of the group, but are quite acceptable inside. Action for the most part has been client-initiated almost from the beginning of the meetings of 1975, and members have come to see themselves not inaccurately as "resident experts" in the eyes of the researcher(s). A number of members have adopted active, more nearly normal roles inside of the group. Aside from those who provide introductions and begin the meetings, certain members have either aided with audio- and videotaping or become involved in the more integral role of peer-counselor, elaborating and clarifying reports of other members on the basis of knowledge gained informally outside of the group or actually providing both support and advice to the member seeking help. In short, the group meetings, by providing a temporary suspension of diminished status and attendant roles of dependency and by providing an open, unregulated, yet confidential setting in which clients can interact as full members, exist as an arena of normalcy for those involved.

2.7. Example 6

Penny:	Jim? I had my birthday party. Got new earrings.
Deac:	You should give some to me.
Rick:	Men wear them too.
Deac:	I know.

Stan: Men wear them all the time. My dad wears one.

Deac: He should get his ears pierced.

((At this point Brad's supervisor enters seeking him. Brad apologizes and goes to work, briefly explaining his new job to Jim Turner. Action then continues:))

Penny: You know what my brother did? In the wine, punch!

Jim T: Did you get drunk?

Penny: Some. Fun.

2.7.1. Eventfulness reporting

The reporting of events, either events in the life of the group member speaking or events in the life of some significant other person, is a relatively common in-group occurrence and a widespread practice among the client population in general.[4] In 44 of the 77 meetings sampled, 81 separate eventfulness reports were made. In a number of these instances, a group member reported a series of events, but only reports of eventfulness as a whole have been counted, some persons contributing torrents of events within a 3-5 minute monologue. Reports of eventfulness in the lives of other persons were made 24 times in 19 of the sampled meetings. Such reports were generally limited to one or two events. In this area the distinction between "me" (my event) and "other" (not my event) is not all that clear, since many clients claim the eventfulness of significant others as their own. In this piece of the transcript, Penny has begun making an eventfulness report of her birthday presents and her birthday party at which there was wine in the punch. She later adds her trip to the San Diego Zoo the previous weekend. The fact that her monologue is broken up by what turns out to be a significant amount of dialogue is not so much indicative of topic changes and return as it is indicative of certain aspects of turntaking within the group meetings.

2.7.2. Turntaking: Getting and holding the floor

At the beginning of the cited bit of transcript, Penny merely says, "Jim?" before beginning her eventfulness report. An *initial request* for the floor, with or without subsequent acknowledgment by researcher or group member, is one means by which one may get his or her "turn." Often arrangements are negotiated beforehand during lunch break for opportunities to "talk in the meeting today." A number of "reservations" are made in this way. Similarly, it is apparent from proceedings in meetings that occasionally clients have at least roughly worked out a plan for providing an opportunity for certain others to talk.

Speaking for others is one rather common way of gaining or obtaining the floor. Often one member will introduce another with such statements as "Jim, Joy has a problem to talk about today." The speaker may have nothing personally to contribute to the discussion except the information about another's problem and the ability to get the floor for that usually more reserved member. Such intercession is witnessed on a regular basis. One may also occasionally speak for another by providing interpretation, by either elaborating or clarifying details of an otherwise sketchy or convoluted report by a fellow member. Likewise, some interpretation is sometimes necessary in the cases of members with rather pronounced speech impediments of one sort or another which certain fellow clients are more competent at understanding. When performing in either of these roles, group members generally make brief entrances into discussion and do not really gain the floor by their actions. One can also gain the floor by invitation, the current speaker introducing another group member into his or her monologue as a means of then handing the floor over to that person. Penny provides this service for Yvette a little further on in this meeting.

Any lull or break in the dialogue is seen as an open invitation to anyone to assume the floor. Many members take turns by "jumping in," interjecting personal statements ostensibly on topic into an ongoing discussion. Often one member gains the fore (if not the floor) in this manner. Topic shifts are quite often realized in this manner as well. An example that emerges from this meeting a little further along in the transcript is where Rick mentions San Francisco in a particular context. Edie uses this reference to mention a trip to San Diego and give her narrative, then Penny breaks in to add her news of a trip to the zoo in San Diego. Somehow action has moved from discussion of Rick's dying grandfather to a recreational venture by Penny. Often quite subtle shifts in both floor and topic are brought about in this way. Interestingly, although some clients are no doubt consciously depending on rather tenuous relationships to make such connections and maneuver for control, others are just as likely simply seeing associations between points and saying what they happen to have been reminded of. Occasionally members have gotten "all talked out" (having exhausted a topic) or had "nothing to talk about," in which cases the researcher has either invited speakers or initiated a topic with relevant questions put to the group as a whole.

Another relatively common phenomenon of turntaking is the *discontinuous monologue*. Certain clients, once they have been acknowledged, will volunteer perhaps one piece of information, after which other members speak and the topic apparently shifts. Other pieces are subsequently added to this original monologue in a series of intermittent interjections which are separated by the ongoing and changing discussion of the rest of the group. Such speakers remain on topic with respect to themselves, but not with respect to the group discussion as a whole. A possible explanation for this dogged commitment to speak one's piece is that many clients enter the meetings and operate according to a "private agenda," having determined beforehand what they will contribute in the meeting, and without intending to interact with the group as a whole.

"Hogging the mike" is a practice that a few members have been able to employ with some success. For some time, an external microphone was utilized and possession of it signaled the right to speak. One woman regularly demanded, "Gimmee that thing! You gotta hear this!" as a means of gaining control of the microphone and then routinely refused to relinquish possession of it. With or without the use of the microphone, this sort of direct and tenacious assault on the floor is one means employed to get and hold the center of group attention. Member status is one more relevant factor in determining possession of the floor. Less popular or more reserved members are often cut short (this happens to Edie in this piece of the transcript) while other, higher status members may speak at length. Variation is extreme regarding this phenomenon: a few clients are almost immediately and rudely interrupted, while others are allowed to go on ad nauseum.

2.8. Example 7

Rick:	My mom is going to the airport Sunday to see my Grandpa. I go with her at 10 o'clock. I'm going with my dad.
Jim T:	Where's your dad going?
Rick:	To the airport to take my mom.
Jim T:	You and your dad are staying here?
Rick:	Mom is going to the airport to see Grandpa. It's important to me. He's been sick a long time. He went to the hospital one time with sun fever. You know, people get sunstroke. People die from it real easy. He passed out. He's blind, he lost his memory, Everything. He's all alone. His wife's gone, died. He's had a hard life. You miss somebody and you love somebody. You know what I mean?
Jim T:	Is he in the hospital?

Rick: No, a convalescent home in San Francisco. It's serious
          important to me. I miss him if he's gone.

2.8.1. *Personal problems at home*

Personal problems at home were reported 76 times in 37 of the meetings sampled. Sickness in the family (such as Rick reports here) and familiar conflicts (divorces, separations, arguments) were most frequently reported, and were reported approximately an equal number of times. There was only one report by a member living with parents of parental restrictiveness, but complaints of overdiscipline and restrictiveness in foster homes were quite common. There were only three reports of having been teased or hit by persons (usually children or teenagers) in the neighborhood. Reports of personal problems at home are generally very upsetting, and highly emotional reactions often interrupt or follow such reports. In the instance above, Rick announces that what he is reporting is important and that it has to do with his grandfather being sick. This explicitly signals to the rest of those in attendance that this is not an eventfulness report. He restresses the seriousness of the matter in his summary statement as well. In general, reports of personal problems at home are given close attention, and support and/or advice is likely to follow. In this case Rick seems to be seeking support which is not forthcoming.

2.8.2. *Explaining problems*

In the example offered here, Rick at first reports his problem without making mention of his grandfather's ill health. After some apparent confusion among members over the nature of his report, he repeats his initial statement about his mother going to the airport to see his grandfather, then adds that this is important, not mere recreation. He then elaborates on his grandfather's sickness, which at first is described as "sunstroke," but with some elucidation of its symptoms appears to be stroke. His grandfather is not in a hospital, but in a convalescent home (and apparently has been for some time), and Rick closes by implying that he might now be dying.

Quite often the presentation of problems such as this is *refined by elaboration*, much in the same way that Rick has done: initial misunderstanding is resolved by more precise, detailed, and understandable statements that emerge gradually. Questions on the part of listeners are commonly a help in eliciting such clarifications. In many instances, an exact knowledge of circumstances in never arrived at by the listeners (e.g., the confusion over the nature of Rick's grandfather's condition). However, in general, speakers are alert to the responses of their listeners and following an apparent miscommunication quite routinely begin to provide a more elaborated version which eventually does enhance the audience's understanding of the problem being reported.

Certain personal problems by their nature evolve over time (e.g., parental separation and divorce, terminal illness). Thus, in some instances explanations *emerge over time* with information being supplied in a serial fashion over a perhaps prolonged period of time as events unfold. However, it is also true that in many cases the speaker has been informed only cursorily or indirectly, or has been given an intentionally simplified explanation by well-meaning relations. In such instances, it may take a number of weeks for a group member to figure out the exact nature of circumstances and events and to provide a coherent explanation to the group. In addition to the problem of having limited access to information, there is also occasionally the problem of the speaker's limited comprehension. Rather clear-cut and even well-explained circumstances can escape the understanding of some group members. Such confusion can certainly slow down or impede the emergence of a coherent explanation. Often, it appears that in such instances, a speaker's *provision of partial information* is in itself an attempt to garner assistance from the group in arriving at a coherent and understandable statement.

Even when the problem and/or its explanation have not emerged over time, explanations are often *supplied piecemeal*, with one or more additional group members contributing to a clarification or elaboration on the basis of information gained outside of the meeting. An example of this cooperative explanation is seen at the beginning of this meeting, where at least three of the group members (Stan, Deac and Edie) share in explaining the nature of Don Snitch's problem. Of course it is quite common as well for a member to provide a clear and concise statement of explanation. However, such reports often can be seen as updates of a larger, more complex, and less understandable problem.

2.8.3. *Resolving problems*

Frequently when a group member does present a problem of some kind, advice is either solicited or volunteered. Solicitation of advice may be either direct or implied by the speaker's statement. Fellow group members are eager, for the most part, to provide assistance. If Turner is addressed directly, in most cases he will redirect the question to the group at large.

Advice of course takes many forms, but the most commonly offered advice for resolving a problem is to "ignore it." In some instances, the implication is a sort of psychic numbing reflected in such statements as "Don't let it bother you" and "Don't get all bent out of shape." More often such advice suggests *avoidance or withdrawal* as a solution. "Just walk away from it (or him or her)!" has been recorded numerous times. Removing oneself from a problem situation is of course not always possible. *Acceptance* is another frequently suggested remedy. Statements like, "There's nothing you can do about it" generally refer to problems at home with a parent, to problems with a supervisor at the workshop, or to another person's problem which is particularly upsetting to the group member reporting it. A typical piece of advice to accept a situation is "Hey! You *got* to do what she says, she's your *mother*!"

Denial of the problem is also a possible means of resolution. One might deny the problematic nature of circumstances by stating that it never happened or, more likely, that it didn't happen "like that." In the former case, the problem is dismissed as a "rumor." In the latter, the problem is subjected to *redefinition*, which beyond functioning in denial of problems is a form of resolution in itself. *Redefinition* of a problem is commonly a group endeavor, aimed at making a problem more understandable and at determining culpability. In many instances, arriving at a measure of understanding of the problem is deemed sufficient for closure (and resolution). Redefinition often serves in the *attribution of blame* as well. Within the workshop client population, little stock is placed in the concept of chance or accident. Thus, when there is a problem, particularly regarding social relations (someone did not greet someone else or bumped into someone while leaving the building), a responsible party and ultimate cause are sought out. Often a rather elaborate reordering of "facts" results in an explanation satisfactory to those involved, if only tenuously credible.

In the process of such redefinitions, members often employ a somewhat unique form of logic whereby they reason from conclusion to proposition. One example should suffice: "Someone stole my lunch today. I think it was Jack 'cause he's always begging and eating off of other people's plates," announced one group member. A number of others then volunteered anecdotal reports of Jack's bad habits at lunch and one man claimed that Mary (a counselor) once caught him. "That does it!" the first man added, "I'm gonna report him! Something's gotta be done about this!" *Invoking authority* in the way just cited (reporting complaints to either a supervisor or counselor) is another very commonly suggested means of resolving one's problems if, of course, the nature of the problem warrants such action. Quite often, simple statements of a problem of sorts followed by some advice is not sufficient to relieve the speaker's concern: more comprehensive "treatment" is then administered via still another group process, peer-counseling.

2.8.4. *Peer-counseling*

Rick's account, presented in the above-cited transcript, seems to be soliciting some support in the problem he reports. Although no one volunteers, either immediately or at any later point in the meeting, Rick may have achieved a sense of having unburdened himself anyway. Within the group meetings, *airing one's problems* is often a sufficient remedy. Beyond the effect of increased understanding noted earlier, sharing one's problem with the group has a cathartic effect. Such comments as "I like to talk about my problems, it gets the pressures off my chest!" and "I feel like getting out in the open!" attest to the beneficial effects of such catharsis in self-disclosure. Often as one group member relates his or her particular problem, another member interjects, "The same thing happened to me!" Such statements are offered often as consolation to the afflicted member, but frequently the speaker, previously silent on the subject, registers surprise that such a problem might occur in someone else's life, adding then a statement of his or her own experience. One may then derive a therapeutic effect from speaking to a passive audience, and group members may derive some therapeutic effect from hearing that others face problems similar to those they face in their own lives.

The *peer-counseling* process often entails a short, but positive personality assessment by the person acting as peer-counselor, a restatement of the problem, and direct advice for resolving it. For example, in response to a fellow client's request for help with a problem that was work-related, one man replied, "I like you Dick, you're a nice person, but you have a bad temper. You got to listen to your supervisor, she's your boss and that's her job." The recipient of this advice vowed to try harder in the future. On another occasion, a woman had complained of fights at home between her parents. The peer-counselor remarked, "Your parents are like fighting lions. You are like a kitten caught in the middle. You need somebody to hold you." A generous and prolonged hug was dispensed and smiles ensued immediately afterward. Peer-counseling of this variety is a means of providing support as well as advice to those in need. Often both are included in the statement of the person filling the role. It is perhaps needless to add that the peer-counselor is paid for the service provided in enhanced self-esteem. Certain persons also function in a more general role of *"social interpreter."* Rather than counseling individuals, these persons shore up or repair the social fabric by "explaining" events in ways that eliminate interpersonal conflicts and reaffirm social harmony.

2.9. Example 8

Edie: I went to San Diego on vacation. And we had a family reunion. I had fun dancing and everything. Then I danced with my friend and got real tired.

Jim T: How'd you get the black eye?

Edie: My cousin. He's strong, he goes to school. I was playing with him, he got mad at me and hit me. Bam! It still hurts. I got black and blue. I cried, it hurt, and his mother told him, "Stop it!" I had a headache too from it.

Penny: You know where I go Sunday morning? Go to the zoo in San Diego. I see you [Yvette] on Sunday. The tiger come out.

2.9.1. *Recurrent problems*

Aside from the notable fact that Edie at first volunteered the "good news" of her fun at the family reunion while neglecting to tell the "bad news" of having been hit in the eye by her cousin, there is another noteworthy element in this piece of the transcript. Previously, Rick had mentioned that his possibly dying grandfather was in a convalescent home in San Francisco. Edie then mentioned San Diego and her affairs. Penny then almost interrupted Edie's account of her black eye to report *her* trip to San Diego. Edie had "jumped into" the conversation. Penny later added a third and fourth piece to her already "discontinuous monologue." Such phenomena have been discussed already. What has not been discussed is problems, like Edie's problem of abuse at home, which are *recurrent*. Over the course of her involvement in group meetings, Edie has mentioned some form of abuse at home on numerous occasions, including teasing, more direct verbal abuse from her brother-in-law, a measure of physical abuse and neglect (reflected in reports of lack of food, etc.), and for some time staff counselors have attempted to have Edie moved to a more suitable setting. Her problems are intermittent and "I get used to it after a while."

Recurrent problems are usually not so dramatic as Edie's, but are a mainstay in the group meeting fare. Kit has a problem every week with Tika being jealous of his speaking to other women. Sue has stated more than once,

"I have new problems every week." On numerous occasions she has complained that her mother "called my stuff junk" (and threatened to clean Sue's room), that she is "all alone" with no friends at the workshop and no one calling her at home, that people will not let her play her harmonica or sing near them. She has been accused of bringing the same problems up again and again, but insists that it is all "new" each time. Jack periodically breaks up with his girlfriend due to the pressure of an overzealous foster mother who claims "she is too old for me." His girlfriend is always upset by this, group members cheer her up, consoling and offering moral support, they give Jack a bit of a talking to, and the couple is reunited. In some cases members, like Edie, have problems which do recur despite attempts at alleviation. In many cases, however, the recurrence of problems can be seen as partially due to a *positive evaluation of problems* which provides attention and support to those affected (see Graffam and Turner 1984).[5]

2.9.2. Persistent problems

Like the rest of humanity, occasionally group members report problems which will not abate, but persist over time, possibly evolving, possibly growing. In May of 1979, Phil reported in a group meeting that his mother had "a lump in her throat." Over the next two years, Phil went through renewed hope after remissions, and renewed despair after discoveries of "the cancer spreading," until May of 1981, when his mother died. The ramifications of her death affect his life to the present.

Pat broke up with Anne ostensibly because she was adversely affecting his bowling score. He soon regretted his action, but Anne would have nothing to do with a reconciliation. Soon Emma entered the fray in defense of Anne and small factions formed. Emma continued to fan the flames with sometimes rather flimsy or downright false accusations long after either Pat or Anne cared to argue. For over ten months the problem was kept alive, until Pat succeeded in arguing that "the whole thing has gotten out of hand" and was disrupting work on the line. For some time afterward, Emma continued half-hearted attempts at keeping Anne's friendship at Pat's expense, but eventually (seems to have) quit.

2.10. Example 9

((Penny has just mentioned having seen Yvette on Sunday))
Jim T: She was there? What were you doing there Yvette?
Deac: Speak up! ((much laughter by the group))

Edie:	Did you have fun?
Penny:	Tiger. Tiger come out.
Yvette:	He's [her boyfriend] got a new bus now.
Jim T:	He got a new bus?
Yvette:	Ya, a brand new bus, a blue one.
Jim T:	Is it one of those very large buses or
Yvette:	A small bus, it's his own bus.
Deac:	It holds 9.
Jim T:	So he can take people around in it.

2.10.1. *Competency claims*

The important as yet undiscussed element of this bit of the transcript is Yvette's well substantiated claim that her boyfriend has just gotten a new bus. This fact reflects positively on Yvette's own status as (more nearly) normal. *Competency claims* of various sorts were made 57 times in 49 of the meetings sampled. *Competency displays*, as exemplified above, are claims which are either substantiated (as Yvette's is here) or at least highly credible. Out of a total of 45 such claims made in the sample, 31 were from the 25 sample meetings held prior to 3/15/78 and only 14 such claims were made in the 52 sample meetings held subsequently. Members of the group during that earlier period were, in general, higher functioning clients, many of whom left the workshop for either competitive employment or a more habilitative work setting. Likewise, many of those earlier members went on to independent living situations, drivers' licenses in some cases, and marriage in a few cases. More recently the general functioning level of clients has been lower, with more clients (and group members) less likely to move to competitive employment, live independently, or ever marry. With a relative paucity of authentic accomplishments that *display* competence, the more recent members have been more active in making competency claims that are obviously *fabricated*.

Normalcy fabrications (Turner 1983) involve claims of a normal life away from the workshop with another job (perhaps in entertainment), a wife or husband and children, a nice house or condo and other amenities of middle class splendor. A number of such claims have been reported both in and out of group meetings. Also common are *grandiose claims of alternate identity*, which involve claims that the speaker is in fact "the *real* Henry Winkler," "a secret agent, James Bond 007," etc. These claims are held to in earnest, often serving as self-defining identities, privately maintained, for long periods of time. This type of fantasizing is distinct from that which serves as a vital form of entertainment (yet to be discussed). Ten or twelve total fabricated claims of competency were found in the meetings held from 3/15/78 through 1982 and only two such claims in the earlier meetings sampled. Competency claims of one sort or another are integral to the self-esteem of many individuals. Instances are widespread both in and out of meetings and the reports in the group meetings are somewhat reflective of these wider group concerns with normalcy and competency, which are to some extent (perhaps erringly) equated.

2.11. Example 10

((The group has been discussing Yvette's boyfriend's new bus and his practice of driving friends around in it.))

Penny: Him fun. Him funny on the bus.
Jim T: What's funny about him? Does he tell jokes or
Yvette   ((Penny echoes)): Mmm. Hmmm. ((indicating "Yes"))
Jim T: He makes everybody laugh, huh? What kind of jokes does he tell? Not dirty jokes I hope. ((tongue in cheek))
Yvette: Ya, some dirty jokes.
Stan: You like dirty jokes? Dirty jokes about ostriches coming out of communist China?
Jim T: Ostriches coming out of communist China? Is there a joke about that?
Stan: No, that's no joke!

2.11.1. *Humor*

Humor plays a very important role at the workshop and in the group meetings as well. Within the workshop client population "fooling around" takes many forms. Although often counted among inappropriate behaviors, name calling can be perfectly acceptable when it involves the right peoople in the right context and carries the proper intonations. "Hey you dirty old man!," "Hey Mama!," or "Okay Daddy I hear you!" are all examples of good natured namecalling which contributes to social relationships and social harmony rather than threatening either. Private or in-group jokes are common as well. One small group of men continued for months telling each other periodically, "Look out behind you, you dynamic scoundrel you!" and various permutations on the theme of surprise attack. Two rather ample men have been observed on a number of occasions bumping bellies in a sort of mock-sumo demonstration. One man who routinely shouts and waves a finger skyward has a repertoire of slogans many of which have cryptic or private meaning. Perhaps his most prevalent is "You're muy loco Kachina, no comprende!" followed by much laughter. When asked what the meaning of the statement might be, he responded "You need a psychiatrist." Insults and other deprecating remarks are sometimes made successfully and in good fun. A number of the staff members often share in good humor with clients. One rainy day clients were permitted to eat in the workshop building itself. The head of production stood at the main entrance into the work area acting as a maitre d', ushering clients to "nice table(s) with a view."

Within the group meetings there is a significant amount of fooling around that goes on as well. Stan's repetitions about "the nation," the group locking Jim Turner out of the room momentarily, and the talk about jokes are all examples from the transcript presented here. On the subject of *jokes*, within the sample of meetings, the incidence of jokes being told is rather low in view of the informality of the group meeting, the desire to approach normalcy, and the relative diversity of topics discussed. The quality of the jokes in the sample makes up for the scarcity. One man having returned from a recent trip to Las Vegas said, "Boy did I have fun in Vegas! Did I have fun in Vegas? You bet your bottom dollar I did!" Another man confessed to having told a number of people at the workshop that Roger, a friend and fellow group member, had "passed away." Hal, one of the most prominent workshop comedians, has delivered a number of "Here's Johnny"-type monologues over the past few years, many suitable for publication in themselves. In one of the meetings sampled, he performed one of these monologues, a story of "Close Encounters of the Weird Kind" in which various workshop outcasts were mimicked, with Hal also playing the role of a comical admonishing parent-figure. Finally, there is this joke about the ostriches which Stan seems to inadvertently play on Jim Turner. It is as cryptic and seemingly self-contradictory as the best Zen Master riddles and Stan sounds serious when he retorts, "That's no joke!" The meaning remains a mystery, but in another meeting in the sample Stan is heard to spontaneously blurt, "Those Chinese detectives are moving in!" If Stan's is a private joke, one can at least join in the hope that the Chinese detectives do not move in disguised as ostriches. It is enough to understand Stan's joke as a venture in playfulness, perhaps as an attempt to initiate some group-constructed fantasy narrative, a phenomenon relatively common to group meetings. Such narratives are usually begun under the guise of one member having had a dream in which certain group members took part. Other members may then join in the construction of a plot. The most popular themes have been the wedding of one group member to another and their subsequent honeymoon (all of which other members are allowed to partake in during this "dream") and food-related extravaganzas of one sort or another. In the sample, Stan is a major contributor to one such *"dream" narrative* where he reports having had a dream in which he had a garden and all the fruits and vegetables turned into people. Various members then ask, "What was I?" and Stan assigns a role to each. Soon a number of other members are making and changing the initial assignments. Hal, the comedian mentioned earlier, has been a promoter and contributor to "dream" narratives on numerous occasions. However the chief "dream weaver" of the workshop and perhaps the person who introduced and inspired the phenomenon is a woman, Julie, whose remarkable imagination would rival that of Rod Serling, Lewis Carroll, or a whole host of cheap opium smokers. Her narratives, often delivered independently of aid from other members, include "The Space Mouse," a violent and dogged salami, trips to outer space where she is "inspected" while naked by the spacemen, etc. The heyday of the "dream" narratives was probably between 1977 and 1979, but occasional attempts crop up after this period, though they occur less often and are less inventive and elaborate.

2.11.2. *Dreams*

Reports of actual dreams are also rather common events in the group meetings. Actual dreams are clearly distinguished from fantasy dream narratives. Instances exist where, when dreams have been reported and then other members have attempted to fictionalize the dream, the dreamer has asserted the authenticity and inalterability of the report. In the sample of 77 meetings, 40 dreams were reported in 21 of the meetings. The distribution is relatively consistent over time. Approximately two-thirds of the dreams reported were "good" dreams, the rest described as "nightmares" or "bad dreams." Examples include Stan dreaming about lying down under a tree with his girlfriend and looking up at the sky, Rick dreaming that he had sex with a pretty girl and saw his brother in a fishtank, Roger dreaming that he was threatened by one of the more aggressive clients at the workshop, and describing his dream as a "nightmare."

To date, over 700 separate dream reports have been collected at the workshop. When Turner began asking clients if they had had any dreams, people were reticent to admit that they did dream. Gradually individuals began to loosen and open up, and the dream reports began to emerge. Within group meetings, dream reports are sometimes solicited (by a simple question as to whether anyone has had any dreams lately) and sometimes volunteered. The gradually increasing disclosure of previously "privatized" aspects of thinking, feeling, and experiencing has been a trend within the group meetings and has been observed in new members as they join and become familiar. In fact, not only dreams, but reports of fantasies ("pretending"), of having "secret" hopes or wishes, of having a "hidden side," of having or being an alternate identity have all come to be admitted/reported more openly as the group experience has evolved.

2.12. How group meetings benefit the members

Aside from benefiting the researcher(s) by providing direct access to individual informants and special insights into phenomena in the larger ethnographic setting, and aside from benefiting other professionals who might be interested in group processes, counseling techniques in general, or in learning how mild and moderately mentally retarded persons think, feel, interact, etc., are there specific ways in which one can say that involvement in group meetings benefits those workshop clients who attend on a regular basis? I say yes.

1. *The non-directive technique and informal style* of the meetings has allowed members to define and determine the course of proceedings, enabling the group meetings to meet the needs of members both immediately and as concerns and the nature of potential problems change over time. At the same time, such "nonstructure" points out the general and focal concerns of the wider social group, making the identification of habilitative needs and client wants somewhat easier.

2. *The independent professional affiliation of the researcher(s)* provides a neutral ground where members can air grievances, voice opinions, report experiences, and express feelings about both the workshop (work, staff, or peers) and home (family, neighborhood, or social life) without any potentially adverse ramifications. For example, if one complains about the workshop at home, a parent or care provider may make trouble back at the workshop by getting involved. Likewise, if one complains at the workshop of some problem at home, a counselor or other staff member may make trouble at home. In the group meetings, one can register any report more or less officially, and yet not risk getting caught in the cross-fire between care providers and workshop staff. There is then no cost or potential cost attached to any statements and a sense of release or resolution is made more likely or more

complete.

3. *The creation of an arena of normalcy* within the context of the group meetings enhances feelings of self-worth in members by creating new status (more nearly normal status) for those members. Members are made to feel like they are the "experts." Members are encouraged to participate in the counseling process (when problems are reported) as "peer-counselors." Since even the events of everyday existence are valued, members are made to feel significant and fully human. On the reverse side of normalcy, members come to see that it is acceptable, even normal, to have problems. Everybody has problems, perhaps even the researcher. The fact that behavior within meetings is primarily unregulated and unreported to staff provides a very definite and probably necessary "time out" from the otherwise dependent and oft-times suppressed existence of daily living as a mentally retarded person.

4. *Confidentiality and developing familiarity* within the group encourages and allows members freedom and safety in increased self-disclosure. The meetings can become a place to talk about more private and personal matters, in many cases matters previously buried in "that part of me nobody knows." Often such disclosures of intimate concerns are matters a person has "wanted to get off my chest" for quite some time.

Perhaps the deepest and most complex of these highly personal concerns pertain to the socio-emotional aspects of being a mentally retarded adult. As Matt has said, "It's hard to be a grown up kid. It's a hard life." In Sue's words, "It's hard to be an adult. I'd like to be free." Dealing with the stigma of handicap is hard enough and has been recognized as one of the four main focal concerns of clients within the workshop population (Turner 1983). But for many clients there is the even greater problem of being caught in a paradoxical dilemma with all the metamessages of a classic doublebind situation. They are constantly being told they are "grown up," yet they remain in a dependent position with relatively little direct control over their lives (something like the politics of childhood). Attendant upon the status of grown up are certain behavioral expectations: one is to act "mature," "like an adult," etc. Yet money is dispensed, relationships are monitored, "adults" are told to clean their rooms and not to "talk back," etc. The group meetings very clearly provide a means and a place for the people who share this unique problem to discuss it together, as well as to discuss the joys and frustrations of being alive and their many shared and similar experiences providing a common ground and a measure of consolation (in numbers). That such persons can laugh about "ostriches coming out of communist China" is a testimony to their resiliency as well as their sense of humor.

3.1. Introduction

Phil, John, and Timmy are employees and clients at a sheltered workshop for mentally retarded adults, the Workshop described in detail by Jim Turner (1983). They are men in their late twenties or early thirties, all suffering from Down's syndrome. Phil has a tested IQ of 44, in the moderately retarded range. While he has a slight speech impediment and neither reads nor writes, he is a fluent conversationalist and occasionally composes poems orally. John's tested IQ is 61, in the mildly retarded range. He reads and writes at the third or fourth grade level, and sometimes acts as a scribe for his friend Timmy. Timmy has a tested IQ of 47, and other clients have some difficulty understanding his thick speech.

For seven years, Turner has been meeting weekly with small groups of Workshop clients to discuss whatever topics the clients wish to raise. This paper examines a conversation which took place among Phil, John, and Timmy during one of these group meetings. It will show what can be learned from such a conversation about Workshop culture and about the competences of retarded adults.

The episode I will examine took place during a group meeting on May 19, 1982. It began with the following exchange, in which Phil, John, and Timmy refer to another workshop client, Randy, who does not participate in the group meetings.[7]

From Episode G:

```
1 Jo:    It says here —
         [                    ]
2 Ph:    I got a question for
3        you two. My question I wanna say
4        is —
```

```
    5  Jo:    Yes?
    6  Ti:    ((sigh))
                 [         ]
    7  Ph:    Uh —
    8           ((calmly)) Is he's your friend,
    9           Randy Roe?
   10  Ti:    Yes.
   11  Jo:    Yes.
                 [    ]
   12  Ph:    Why?
```

In this exchange, Timmy and John have asserted their friendship with Randy, while Phil has challenged it.

The episode ends a few minutes later with this interchange between Phil and John, interrupted briefly by another client, Lucille. Again, the topic is Randy.

G:

```
  170  Ph:    An' that's what he's
  171           tryin' to do: get me
                 [                    ]
  172  Jo:    Uh, Philly?
  173  Ph:    in trouble.
  174  Lu:    (                    )
                 [                    ]
  175  Jo:    Sometimes he got —
  176           he got me in big trouble, too.
```

And John tells a story about how John got blamed when Randy scratched up his brother's pants.

I intend to ask very simply what was going on in this episode. "What was going on?" is *the* ethnographic question. Applied here to a very brief strip of experience, it can lead to an understanding of Workshop Society far beyond the single episode.

What seems to have gone on, from the beginning to the end of this episode, is a change of heart on John's part regarding his erstwhile friend Randy. In line G:11 Johns asserts that Randy is his friend; by line G:176 he is distancing himself from Randy by describing how Randy once got him in "trouble." Furthermore, John's "conversion" from a pro-Randy to an anti-Randy stance is prompted and, as we shall see, promoted throughout by fellow client Phil. Thus at one level, to ask what is going on here is to ask what Phil is doing to manipulate John's position and what John does to respond to those moves.

However, to understand Phil's strategies we must not only examine what he says and does in this conversation, but understand norms he cites, concepts he refers to, and techniques he applies which are peculiar to Workshop Society. An explanation of what is going on must refer to the cultural context within which this episode takes place. Turner (1983) and Turner, Kernan, and Gelphman (1984) have described many cultural features of Workshop Society. As part of this analysis, I will refer to these as well as to unpublished ethnographic observations made by Turner, myself, and our research colleagues.

The more cultural background we understand when reading the transcript of this conversation, the more it will become clear that John's "conversion" is not the only thing going on in this episode. Beneath the surface, I will argue, John's change of heart resolves a hidden conflict between him and his friend Timmy.

Moreover, as we come to understand John's goals, Phil's strategies, and the cultural background to this conversation, more and more of Phil, John, and Timmy's comments will make sense. We will be in a better position to distinguish true lapses in logical thinking from utterances which may sound odd but are interactionally successful. Thus this study, narrow in focus as it is, will provide usable data about the competence of retarded adults. Moreover, these two themes — Workshop culture and clients' competence — will prove to be closely intertwined.

3.2. Sources of the data

The ethnographic information to be cited here is based on seven years of weekly visits to the sheltered workshop by Jim Turner, as well as long periods of participant-observation by Turner's colleagues, especially Joe Graffam. In addition, I draw on my own observations made during weekly visits over a three-month period which included the day of the group meeting analyzed here.

The group meetings are always audiotaped, and are frequently videotaped as well by researcher Frank Marlowe. Clients have given their consent for these tapes to be used for research purposes. The May 19 meeting discussed here was videotaped not only by Marlowe's roving camera, but by two stationary cameras positioned to record the speech and actions of almost all participants.[8] The transcript in Appendix B was made using both the videotapes and the audiotaped record.

3.3. Background

Before even beginning to examine the details of the conversation in which John was "converted," the reader will need extensive background information regarding the Workshop, the group meetings, and the kinds of problems discussed in them.

3.3.1. *The workshop*

About two hundred clients/employees put in a seven-hour day at the workshop doing light manufacturing jobs. The clients range in age from 18 to 55, and their IQs range from 29 to 75. The average client IQ is 50, meaning that most of the clients are considered "moderately" mentally retarded, i.e., "trainable." Most of the clients are Anglo, reflecting the population of the local community, and 60 percent are male (Turner 1983).

The Workshop is unusual compared to most settings in which retarded adults spend their lives. Since the move toward de-institutionalization, many mildly retarded adults live on their own in the community, but they are usually marginal members of "normal" society. Some of them are preoccupied with hiding the stigma of retardation (Edgerton 1967; Edgerton and Bercovici 1976), and few of them enjoy satisfying friendships with their non-retarded peers. In contrast, Workshop clients spend the day with others who are more or less retarded like themselves, and thus most of them are able to carry on more normal social relationships (Turner 1983). At the same time, the Workshop does not place clients in as dependent and controlled a situation as large groupings of the retarded in institutions are liable to. The Workshop counseling staff operates on the assumption that at least some clients will move on someday to independent employment. Therefore the staff deliberately promotes a degree of autonomy among the clients, letting clients interact freely during breaks, lunchtime, and even on the shop floor to the extent that production is not impeded. It is the gathering of a large group of retarded peers in this relatively unconstrained atmosphere which permits clients to conduct a rich social life among themselves.

3.3.2. *The group meeting*

I am concerned with the resolution of peer conflict and what it can tell us about the cognitive and social skills of Workshop clients. As neo-Vygotskian theorists in psychology point out, we can't talk about cognitive skills except in reference to the "activity" in which they are embedded (e.g., Wertsch 1981). This is an especially important point here, for the "activity" within which Phil and John's conversation took place — the group meeting — is an unusual one, even within the unusual setting of this sheltered workshop.

"Activity" refers to the socio-cultural definition of what people are doing at a given time and place. It includes the actors' goals, the culturally legitimate means for achieving the goals, and constraints on the actors' behavior (Cole 1983). In this section, I will describe the "activity" of the group meeting as it is defined by the researchers and the clients who participate in it. I will also indicate their main goals, and suggest the ways in which they normally carry on the meeting (their "means"). Later, in analyzing the conversation, I will refer to a number of Workshop norms which function, along with more obvious limitations like the dependent status of retarded adults, as constraints on the clients' behavior in the group meeting.

During the course of the day, clients are periodically excused from work to participate in classes, meetings with their counselor, or an occasional sports activity. The group meeting is one such scheduled non-work activity in which designated clients participate. About a dozen clients sit around a large table in a conference room and hold an hour-long discussion with Jim Turner and other researchers. At the time of this study, three separate groups were meeting. This paper concerns the "12:00 group," the set of clients who met from noon to 1:00 every Wednesday. Two other groups met every other week, on alternate Wednesdays, from 2:00 to 3:00.

Turner, a psychologist, began offering the group meetings in 1975 as a service to the Workshop to reciprocate for the opportunity to do ethnographic research there. At first, the staff requested that certain "troublemakers" among the clients be made to participate in the meetings, but those clients have since left, and participants are now essentially self-selected. That is, many clients have volunteered that they would like to participate in a group meeting, and when there is an opening because a participant leaves the Workshop or chooses to quit the group, Turner fills the opening from this waiting list. The only constraint on participation is that the staff may request that a client who already participates in many classes or other activities not be allowed to take part in a group meeting as well (Turner, personal communication). Openings are infrequent, and many of the same clients have been participating in the group meetings for years.

What makes the group meetings different from classes and other

organized activities is that Turner and his researcher-colleagues have structured the group meetings as an opportunity for participants to discuss among
themselves whatever is on their minds. Turner encourages participants to set
their own agenda, which they do either by taking the floor during the meeting, or by putting in a request to one of the researchers ahead of time (e.g.,
"Tell Jim [Turner] I want to talk in the meeting today"). For the researchers,
the groups also serve a secondary purpose as a research setting. As mentioned, all participants have given informed consent for the group meetings
to be recorded and analyzed. In addition to studying naturally occurring discussion, as I do in this paper, Turner or other researchers may occasionally
use the group meetings to pose a particular topic for research purposes, e.g.,
asking for dream reports.

Clients essentially agree with researchers about the goals of the group
meeting. When asked to explain the purpose of the session to a new participant or new researcher, their definition predictably conforms to that offered
by Phil on June 2: "We come in here about 12:00 to 1:00, and we discuss our
problems in this meeting, like at home and at work ...." He noted the researchers' function as well, saying, "Jim and Joe ask us a question, what is right
and wrong question, and that's why they present their (blue outline); it's on
(that red) book."[9] Other clients added that they sometimes discuss dreams,
poems, jokes, marriage, and sex, and Phil summed up: "We talk about *anything* ... in here." Indeed, the researchers have found that topics taboo
elsewhere are more likely to come up within group meetings (Turner, Kernan, and Gelphman 1984).

It is interesting to note one small difference in perception. While researchers refer to the sessions as the "group meeting" or simply the "group" (em-
phasizing, perhaps, the resemblance to group therapy sessions), clients
almost always say simply the "meeting." This subtle difference suggests that
clients de-emphasize any possible psychotherapeutic aspect of the session,
and emphasize the high status associated with being a participant — perhaps
a status associated in some way with business meetings or conferences.

Not only do clients talk about "anything" in the group meetings, but over
the course of seven years they have learned to talk to one another directly,
and to look to one another for advice rather than seeking direction from the
researchers/counselors. This direct interaction is nicely illustrated in the
appended transcript. It is true that the researchers' presence still shapes the
conduct of the meeting. On many occasions researchers intervene spontaneously or get invitations to intervene, which they may decline or accept. How-

ever, Turner and his colleagues have made a consistent, deliberate effort to guide clients toward finding solutions and giving advice on their own. After hearing a client state a problem, they often turn to a neutral party and ask, "What advice would you give?" or turn to an involved party and ask, "Is that how you see the problem?" Clients who might not have offered advice or their perceptions spontaneously do so when thus prodded. In the group meetings, then, one often observes clients functioning in their "zone of proximal development," accomplishing with the guidance of the researchers (or more capable clients) what they could not accomplish entirely on their own (see Wertsch 1979). Little by little, clients so guided take on more and more ability to resolve peer conflicts, at least within the group meeting, independently.

Phil is the outstanding example of a client who has learned the role of peer counselor. Although Phil is illiterate and operates as a "Loner" on the shop floor (Turner 1983), the researchers noticed special talents in him, including his ability to compose oral poetry. They deliberately encouraged Phil to give advice during group meetings, and he now does so loquaciously and often spontaneously. As will be seen in the example I will analyze, other clients cede him the floor and take his pronouncements seriously. Phil has come to see himself as a counselor-in-training; indeed, in the June 9 meeting, he referred to himself as a "psychiatrist," a term clients usually reserve for Jim Turner.

3.3.3. *Kinds of problems*

Most of the conversation I will analyze concerned a particular kind of problem which came up frequently in group meetings, a problem I will refer to as "taking sides." It is important to understand the issue of "taking sides," especially because it is the kind of problem which clients raise in group meetings but do not take to their counselors, who do not consider it a "real" problem (Turner, personal communication). In order to put "taking sides" into context, as well as to give a better sense of what group meetings are about, I will digress here to outline the other kinds of problems raised by clients during the meetings.

To get a sense of what kinds of problems are salient to clients, I noted every problem during any group meeting from May 5, 1982, through August 11, 1982, when I was making weekly visits to the workshop. It was not always easy to decide what to count as a problem, and if other fieldworkers tried to code the same set of group meetings, they would probably come up with slightly different lists. I tried to include any announcement of a situation

about which the announcer seemed to be genuinely upset, as opposed to
announcements which were made just for the sake of passing on news. Even
using this rough criterion, problems were difficult to count. Sometimes a
client would talk for a long stretch during the meeting, and I had to decide
whether the entire discourse concerned only one or more than one problem.
Sometimes a client would bring up a problem again later during the meeting;
this I did not count as a new instance.

I grouped similar problems together, coming up with twenty-two
categories, many of them closely related to each other. Table 1 groups the
kinds of problems and indicates the frequency with which they were mentioned during the thirteen weeks covered.

Table 1. Kinds of Problems Discussed in Group Meetings, 5/5-8/11

PEER PROBLEMS (Total: 79)	Frequency
With intimates	
Taking sides.	24
(See explanation below)	
Problems within friendships.	7
E.g., Sara complains that Nancy "broadcast" the news of her father's death; Alan complains that a friend was begging food from him.	
Break-ups or serious problems in a romance.	6
E.g., A new acquaintance declined to be David's girlfriend; John considers breaking up with Jenny.	
The complaint: "X is trying to break up Y and Z."	5
E.g., Marie complains that Leslie told her that Phil has a second girlfriend.	
Conflicts with a housemate.	6
E.g., Norman had an argument with his housemate; Phil is worried that his roommate has changed since his operation.	
With others	
The complaint: "X is bugging me."	13
E.g., Marie: "Manny picks on me on the line."; Alan: "Clarence was bugging me."	

Impersonal complaints about another's behavior. 9
  E.g., Alan complains about Saul's behavior at the bowling
        alley;
        Ralph complains that a client is undressing himself on the
        line.
General ("they") problems on the line. 2
  Marie: "There's too much noice on the line;"
  Toby: "I was roasting and they kept turning the fan away
          from me."
Conflicts which go beyond being "bugged." 2
  Ralph is mad at Herb;
  Ralph and Mitchell have a conflict on the line.
The complaint, "X got mad at me for ...." 2
  E.g., Someone got mad at Timmy for bringing a radio on the
        Workshop bus.

Here and now

Immediate conflict with another group participant. 3
  E.g., Martha thinks Carol wants her to leave the group
        meeting.

TROUBLE (a category bridging peer and authority conclict; Total: 2)

The statement: "I got in trouble." 2
  John: "I accidentally hit Randy with a tree.";
  John: "I got in trouble because of Timmy's asking to take a bite
          of my chicken; it wasn't Timmy's fault."

AUTHORITY (Total: 9)

Problems with counselors, supervisors, houseparents, aides. 6
  E.g., Phil: "Our housemother won't let us run a car wash.";
        Alan's supervisor gets upset when Alan leaves the line.
Frustration regarding rotation from one line to another. 4
  E.g., Jack didn't like working in the kitchen.

OTHER KINDS OF PROBLEMS (Total: 20)

Concern about someone who is sick, injured, or in trouble.	6

    E.g.,   Jack's sister is in the hospital;

              The guys are worried about their houseparent, who

              broke his toe and is depressed.

Distress about death (recent or not).	2

    Martha is upset about her father's death;

    Norman had an upsetting dream about his dead grandmother.

Concern about a news story.	1

    Jack is upset about Reagan's being shot.

Worry about family problems.	3

    E.g.,   Jenny is upset that her sister is drinking.

Conflict with one's family.	2

    Lucille's mom calls her things "junk";

    Norman says his grandfather doesn't love him anymore.

Personal health.	2

    E.g.,   Anne is worried about a foot operation she must have.

Desire for personal improvement.	1

    Timmy wants to change his life.

Practical problems.	3

    E.g.,   The city bus sometimes passes clients by;

              Alan's lunch was "stolen."

    As is clear from the table, the bulk of problems raised in the group meetings are various kinds of peer conflicts (79 out of 110, or over 70 percent, based on this rough count). The only other categories which show up with much frequency are conflicts with authority figures and concern about someone who is sick, injured, or in trouble.

    Turner (1983) discusses the clients' concern with peer conflicts in depth. He notes the clients' need to balance two very important values of Workshop Society: On the one hand, clients desire social harmony; on the other hand, they fear boredom and like to see a certain level of "eventfulness" in their lives. Thus when peer conflict becomes a topic of discussion in the group meeting, participants work hard to resolve the conflict and restore harmony (see also Turner, Kernan, and Gelphman 1984). Yet a certain degree of peer conflict to be discussed confidentially in the group meetings certainly makes the meetings more interesting, and may be one of the reasons that so many clients would like to participate in the groups.

3.3.4. *"Taking sides"*

One kind of problem which especially lends itself to the manufacture of "eventfulness" is the issue I have labeled "taking sides." This is the kind of problem with which clients are concerned in the conversation I will analyze.

"Taking sides" is not exactly an emic term — clients do not actually use it to label this particular kind of problem. However, they do occasionally make a statement of the type, "I don't know what side I want to be on" (John, 6/2), or, "I'm gonna be on X's side" (John, line L:21 in Appendix B). Such statements refer to the shifting pattern of alliances within two specific networks of clients. One network, that with which I will be concerned, involves several participants in the 12:00 group meeting. A second network in which sides are taken involves some participants in one of the 2:00 meetings. The twenty-four separately counted problems listed in Table 1 under "taking sides" actually represent incidents in one of these two continuing sagas: who, in the 12:00 group, will be on what side in the conflicts within their network, and who in the 2:00 group will be on what side of their respective alliances?

About a dozen clients participate in the 12:00 group, and of these, the following six get embroiled, directly or indirectly, in the question of "taking sides": John and his girlfriend Jenny, Timmy, Lucille, Marie and her boyfriend Phil. Clients who are associated with the disputes but who do not participate in the group meetings include Randy Roe, Sandra Castle, Leslie, and several others.

Randy is a symbol of the on-going dispute. Usually, at least within the group meeting, the involved clients express their conflicts in terms of siding with or against Randy. That is, to identify their position within the network, clients will indicate that they are either on friendly terms or on unfriendly terms with Randy, or with a person indisputably allied with Randy, such as his current girlfriend.

One might well ask whether it is worthwhile to analyze in this paper a problem which concerns only a dozen or so clients out of the Workshop population of some two hundred. In a sense, the problem is atypical of peer conflicts, for it seems to have no permanent solution. No sooner is one conflict within this network repaired, than another breaks out between different members, and the involved clients again take sides. However, the problem does bear investigation for several reasons. First, if the bulk of the problems discussed in the group are peer problems, this is the peer problem par excellence. Second it concerns some of the most prominent members of the Workshop community; for instance, Turner reports (personal communication) that John's friendship is highly prized by other clients. Third, almost half the participants in the 12:00 meeting are involved in the continuing disputes, and of these, Phil, John, and Lucille are particularly adept at holding the floor. This means that, except when researchers intervene to encourage other group members to speak, there is a strong chance that the issue of "taking sides" will be discussed in every 12:00 meeting.

3.4. John shifts sides

3.4.1. *The context of John's "conversion"*

On May 19, John entered the group meeting on Randy's side. By the end of the meeting he had denounced Randy. Before discussing how this "conversion" came about, let me put it into its local historical perspective. Jim Turner suggested I use the format of soap opera synopses, since several participants in the conflict are fans of *Dallas* and *Dynasty* and like to see their own conflicts as parallel in some sense to those television dramas. Note in these synopses that because researchers are usually present only one day a week at the Workshop, we sometimes remain ignorant of developments which occur during the intervals between group meetings.

May 5. John is ambivalent about Randy; he reports accidentally hitting Randy with a tree branch, for which he got in trouble. John was also punished because Randy dragged John's foster brother in the dirt. John proposes to leave the Workshop, which would incidentally resolve his dilemma of whether to break up with Jenny. The others are noncommittal.

May 12. John, Timmy, and even Phil argue that Randy Roe and Sandra Castle are indeed cousins (and therefore justified in demonstrating affection, even though Sandra is a married woman); they criticize Lucille for claiming otherwise. Lucille feels "left out," isolated in the anti-Randy camp.

May 19. Again, Lucille feels "left out" and blames Randy for "taking anger out" on her. John and Timmy issue a joint statement defending Randy against the person who is spreading "rumors" about him, and argue that the guilty party is Penny Cole. Phil challenges John and Timmy's friendship with Randy (arguing in the process that Randy and Sandra are *not* cousins). Eventually John renounces Randy while reaffirming his friendship with Timmy.

May 26. Despite last week's "conversion," John again enters the meeting on Randy's side. Lucille, too, has made peace with Randy, but Timmy is in open conflict with him. Phil again challenges John's friendship with Randy, and John again renounces Randy. Lucille, suddenly isolated on Randy's side, tries to blame Timmy for doing "something nasty," but Phil blames Randy instead. Phil and John criticize Lucille for claiming that Randy and Sandra are cousins. Lucille half-heartedly agrees to side with John and the rest against Randy.

June 2. Again despite his prior "conversion," John enters the meeting on Randy's side. Phil is upset that John and Jenny are avoiding him, and implies that they have "blabbed" to Randy about Phil's confidential attacks on him in the meetings. John weeps while Jenny counters with an attack on Timmy, and Lucille lines up with John and Jenny against Phil and Timmy. Phil concedes that Timmy "acts like a kid" and admits, "Maybe I am wrong about Randy Roe." Phil and John reconcile, leaving Timmy isolated.

June 9. Lucille has had a conflagration with Randy, who took away her harmonica when she irritated him with it. Not only Phil, but also John, Timmy, and Jenny support her against Randy. Since everyone is united, there is little discussion about "taking sides" in this meeting.

June 16, 23, and 30. Phil continues to support Lucille in her brief against Randy, but Timmy, John and Jenny have defected back to Randy's side. Lucille is bitter.

July 7 and following weeks. During the week, Lucille and Phil have won Timmy, John, and Jenny back to their side in the anti-Randy camp. Everyone remains opposed to Randy during the summer weeks while various individuals leave for brief vacations. Lucille continues to complain about the harmonica incident, but with everyone in the meeting united, interest fades for the time being in the issue of "taking sides."

In this continuing saga, John's position vis-a-vis Randy was particularly unstable. He switched sides every week or two, and for two meetings in a row, he was persuaded to denounce Randy only to return the following week back on Randy's side.

Given John's frequent shifts, part of asking what went on in the May 19 meeting will be to ask in what sense John was "converted" at all. Did he undergo a cognitive change, a change in the way he perceived the world? If so, did the new perception of the world which Phil developed with him at the interpsychological level (specifically, the perception that Randy would get him in "trouble") get internalized, i.e., become intrapsychological (Wertsch 1979)? Or did it remain at the interpsychological level, maintained only as long as John remained under Phil's influence within the group (cf. Hood, McDermott, and Cole 1981)? Indeed, is it possible that John underwent no cognitive change at all, but simply changed his behavior, "mouthing" a renouncement of Randy for the sake of that highly valued social harmony within the group meeting?

3.4.2. *The May 19 meeting*

John's May 19 "conversion" must be understood not only in light of his switching sides from week to week, but also within the context of other topics discussed during that particular meeting.

The meeting began a few minutes after 12:00 and lasted about an hour. The twelve clients present were John, Jenny, Timmy, Norman, Lucille, Daniel, Phil, Marie, Joan, Mitchell, Nancy, and Alan. Four researchers participated: Jim Turner and Joe Graffam occasionally took part in the discussion, Frank Marlowe operated the cameras, and I took notes without much active participation.

I have identified twelve main episodes during the meeting, each representing a period of talk by one main speaker, usually on a single topic. In

Table 2, these are labeled with letters of the alphabet, and the approximate length of each episode is given.

Table 2. Episodes in the May 19 Meeting

Entry
Starting the meeting

A	Daniel talks about problems at his Home.	10 minutes
B	Phil responds and offers a poem.	4 minutes
C	Marie complains about Penny Cole.	2 minutes
D	Phil complains that his group home was not permitted to hold a car wash. Norman and John comment.	23 minutes
E	Lucille complains about being isolated, with an aside about having a new boyfriend. She allows Phil and John to name Randy Roe and Penny Cole as the causes of her isolation.	3 minutes
F	John reads a speech dictated by Timmy and then extemporizes, complaining that Penny Cole is spreading "rumors" about Randy Roe.	2½ minutes
G	Phil attacks John's friendship with Randy and eventually persuades John that Randy will "get him in trouble."	5½ minutes
H	John begins an attack on Penny Cole. Jim Turner cuts him off to give the floor to Norman.	½ minute
I	Norman describes his dream about his deceased grandmother.	2 minutes
J	Phil responds with a dream about his deceased mother.	2½ minutes

Meeting gradually dissolves as:

K	Alan complains that Clarence bugged him.	2 minutes
L	John renounces Randy.	1 minute
	Post-meeting talk.	

We shall be concerned with Episode G of the meeting. As the table indicates, this episode began three-quarters of the way through the session. However, the question of "taking sides" vis-a-vis Randy, broached openly in

Episode G, was already foreshadowed in three previous episodes. Randy was first mentioned by Timmy in an aside during Episode C, when Marie was complaining about Penny Cole. Much later, at the end of Episode E, Lucille arranged for Randy to become a topic discussion and part of her technique in getting Randy's name on the floor was to refer to Timmy's prior comment. Once Lucille introduced Randy as a topic, John and Timmy began a discussion (Episode F) of their own concerns revolving around Randy.

In Episode G, as we have seen, Phil broke into their discussion to challenge their friendship with Randy. By the end of Episode G, John displayed an apparent "conversion" from pro-Randy to anti-Randy. The subject of Randy was dropped from that point until the meeting was breaking up. Then, in Episode L, John renounced Randy without ambivalence: "I am gonna make my own decision about Randy Roe. I'm not gonna talk to him no more."

3.4.3. *Phil's moves in "converting" John*

At one level, at least, John's "conversion" took place in response to a series of moves by Phil.[10] Thus one approach to the question, "What was going on here?", is to answer the question, "What was Phil doing?" A complete answer to that question would require an analysis of what was really being said and what was really being done during the five and a half minutes of Episode G. However, Labov and Fanshel (1977) spent five years writing a book-length analysis of five minutes of a therapy session. We will have to settle instead for a few illustrations. Before looking at these illustrations, though, the reader is urged to read through the entire transcript of Episode G in Appendix B, to get a sense of Phil's style and the pattern of his interaction with John and other clients.

Demolishing premises. Phil's first attack, beginning on line G:12, is through argumentation and logic, with reference to norms for behavior which are frequently cited at the Workshop. Randy's name has already been the topic of discussion for several minutes, and Phil has already taken the floor and established a clear starting pointing by arranging for Timmy and John to state explicitly that Randy is their friend, i.e., that they are on Randy's side. Now four times in succession, in line G:12, in lines G:21-22, in lines G:26-27, and in lines G:38-39, Phil asks them to justify this friendship with Randy.

When John first takes up the challenge and offers a justification for being Randy's friend, Phil immediately attacks his premise:

G:
12 Ph: Why?
13 Jo: Why? Because we been to skrool with him.
14 Ph: "*Screwed*"?
15 Jo: School.
16 Al?: School.
17 Lu: Goin' to school together.
18 Ph: ((more derisively)) *I* don't care who he go to school with you.
19 Jo: Oh. Kay.

Phil is not just stating a personal preference in line G:18. He is making reference to a norm which I have heard cited several times by the researchers — that it is not legitimate to use long-past relationships as the grounds for current behavior. (For example, Jim Turner cited this rule in the June 2 meeting when trying to circumvent a break between John and Timmy.) In line 19, with his broken "okay," John apparently agrees to the appropriateness of the norm Phil has cited. His reference to school ties has been thrown out, and Phil is free to raise the question "Why?" again, on lines G:21-22. He inserts it within a brief interlude of invective against Randy, which I will mention below.

John makes a response on line G:25 which I was unable to transcribe. Perhaps Phil could not make it out either, for he simply repeats his challenge to John's premises:

G:
26 Ph: Why you runnin' around with him
27   all the time?
28 Jo: Because, because his girlfriend
29   told me —
30 Ph: ((more vehemently)) *I* don't care
31   Leslie think. Leslie is not a boss.
32 Jo: Leslie told me that she wants me to
33   go with Randy Roe, not Timmy.
34 Ph: Don't listen t'her — (to her).
35   ((speechifying)) *You* got a mind for
36   your own, *Timmy* got a mind for his
37   own. (pause)

John can hardly get a justification out of his mouth in lines G:28-29 before

Phil again attacks his premise. Phil argues that John and Timmy have minds of their own, and therefore ought to make their own decisions. They should not let someone else — in this case, Randy's girlfriend Leslie — tell them what to do.

This norm, that one should make up one's own mind rather than following the directives of others, is very commonly heard at the Workshop. Indeed, we have seen that John cites it in Episode L. The word "boss" is an insulting epithet, and to be "bossy" is the oppposite of being "nice" in Workshop parlance (Turner, personal communication).

According to other ethnographers, John has a habit of attributing his own behavior to other people, whether a fellow client, a counselor, his foster mother, or someone else. Nonetheless, he seems to cede rapidly to Phil's argument here. He makes no defense along the lines that "he has to" or "can't help" doing what Leslie says. Apparently such an argument would not hold up against the strong Workshop norm of being one's own boss. After the pause at line G:37, which John does not fill, Phil is at liberty to repeat his challenge for the third time: "And why you two wanna make friends with him?" As I will discuss below, John does not even attempt a response this time.

I have pointed to this section of the transcript to highlight Phil's use of logic: John's premises conflict with norms to which John agrees as a member of the Workshop; therefore his premises do not hold; therefore, he has no grounds for friendship with Randy. However, I cannot leave his sequence without also making a reference to certain of Phil's rhetorical flourishes. First, in lines G:13-14, John mispronounces the word "school" as "skrool," and Phil repeats in exaggerated tones, "*Screwed*?" The researchers present are inclined to doubt that Phil misheard John as saying "screwed." Rather, we suspect that Phil took this opportunity to insert a taboo word (Turner, Kernan, and Gelphman 1984) to attract attention, and subtly to get across the message that hanging around with Randy is likely to get a person "screwed."

Secondly, Phil gradually builds up a dramatic tone of derision and vehemence in his speech, as I have tried to indicate in the transcript. The emphasis in his intonation is pointed. He speaks slowly, with rhythmic pauses between sentences, and increases notably both in pitch and loudness on emphasized words: "*I* don't care who he go to school with you" (line G:18); "*I* don't care (what) Leslie think" (lines G:30-31); "*You* got a mind for your own, *Timmy* got a mind for his own" (lines G:36-37).

Finally, the repetition itself of the question "Why?" is a powerful rhetorical tool. Phil hammers at John's defenses once, and again, and a third time, and a fourth, until they give way.

Restructuring perception of Randy. Another of Phil's persuasive techniques is to portray Randy in such an unfavorable light that John will not want to be associated with him. Apparently most of the clients except Phil consider Randy to be an acceptable friend. However, Phil introduces two themes designed to restructure that perception. He maligns Randy's general behavior as immature, and he argues the specific point that Randy is bound to get John and Timmy into "trouble."

Phil begins to establish the first point in line G:20, in which the transcribers think he says, "I'm — I feel like (he actin' very stubborn baby)." "He," of course, is Randy. If Phil did indeed use the word "baby," it was a serious insult in Workshop parlance. Phil returns to his general criticism of Randy's behavior in lines G:45-57:

G:
47 Ph: *I* don' like (the way) he's acting.
48   To me he acts so big he not — he
49   not — he's not (alive).
50   He say, ((mocking imitation))
51   "*I* got *mus*cles" ((imitating
52   Randy showing his biceps)).
53   He hasn't.
54   He think (he Mr. Big in)
55   that line.

Here Phil mocks behavior which, if Randy really did it, could have been perceived in a positive light by other candidates. It is not undesirable to have muscles, nor is it necessarily unacceptable to display them. However, Phil has used tone of voice and exaggerated gesture to recast this alleged act on Randy's part into a blatant showing off, something *not* acceptable by Workshop norms. Later, in lines G:128-133, Phil escalates his vilification of Randy by claiming — and acting out the claim — that Randy makes faces like a fish. If Phil persuades his audience that Randy really has behaved in the undignified and childish ways Phil has portrayed, they will see Randy's friendship as less desirable, and John will feel the pressure of "public opinion" to disassociate himself from Randy.

Interestingly, Phil links his first two unpleasant portraits of Randy with the concept that Randy will get John and Timmy in "trouble" (lines G:23-24 and lines G:45-46). He does not explain what Randy's alleged babyish behavior might have to do with getting other clients in "trouble." The propensity for getting people in "trouble" seems here to be simply part of the negative portrait Phil seeks to paint of Randy's behavior. However, as we shall see below, the concept of "getting in trouble" turns out to be the axis on which Phil's "conversion" of John revolves. I will discuss the Workshop notion of "trouble" further below.

Mitigating criticisms. Now I will point out a technique which falls more under the heading of "social skill" than "cognitive strategy."

In lines G:1-42, as I have shown, Phil has made a very strong attack on John and Timmy's position. By criticizing their friendship with Randy, Phil has indirectly questioned their own integrity and good sense. He has left John speechless (line G:40), and by the end of the attack, Timmy has pointedly turned away from the table (line G:42). But immediately after this attack, in line G:43, Phil changes his tone and says, "I *like* you two." John ends his silence to respond, "Thank you," and Phil continues, "I really do."

The other researchers have noted this strategy of mitigation many times in the group meetings, especially on Phil's part. They refer to it as the "I like you but — " tactic. (It seems to be related to the general phenomenon of disagreement, "Yes, but —.") Through this tactic a client asserts friendship with the person he is attacking, and reassures that person that he is "a good person," "a nice guy," and so on. In this way, the one criticized is in less of a position to harden himself completely against everything the attacker says. Thus after Phil has re-established more cordial relations between himself and John, if not Timmy, he can expect John to be more open to the restructured perception of Randy which immediately follows.

Phil provides a more elaborate example of the technique in lines G:61-74. In this case, his affirmation of friendship and good feelings toward Timmy and John follow rather than precede any attack on their position. He is lightening the mood after a dramatic and angry tirade against Randy.

G:

61	Ph:	I — I like Timmy. Timmy's a nice
62		person.
63		An' you, too.
64	Jo:	Thank you.
65	Ph:	An' Jenny's a nice (.)
66		((grinning, speeding up))
67		sexy gal.

```
68 Na, others:   ((laugh))
69
70 Jo:      Well, I know she is.
71 Ph:      An'Marie is, too.
72 Na:      ((murmer))
73 Ph:      Sexy and
74          (        ). ((pinching Marie))
```

As before, background knowledge will help the reader understand Phil's techniques here. He refers to Jenny in line G:65 because Jenny is John's girlfriend and, by an implicit rule that girlfriends will side with their boyfriends, is presumed to be aligned with John. A token of friendship to her is a token of friendship to John, as long as there is no threat to John's and Jenny's romantic ties. As a matter of fact, Phil would seem to be in danger of making John jealous by mentioning in line G:67 that Jenny is a "sexy gal." However, "sexy" is a taboo word in Workshop Society (Turner, Kernan, and Gelphman 1984), and Phil suggests by his brief pause, his grin, and the speeding up of his rhythm that he is playing the phrase "sexy gal" primarily to titillate and amuse his audience. The laughter which follows indicates that he has succeeded. There is still the danger that his comment will be read as a flirtation with Jenny; but Phil reduces the danger by balancing this mention of Jenny with a mention in lines G:71-74 of his own girlfriend, Marie.

Holding the floor. One of Phil's most important skills in accomplishing John's "conversion" is his ability to hold the floor and keep the group focused on the topic he had introduced, namely, John's friendship with Randy. An otherwise bizarre exchange between Phil and Lucille, which begins just at the point in the transcript where the last example ended, can be explained as an example of Phil's skill:

```
G:
73 Ph:      Sexy and
74          (        ). ((pinching Marie))
            [                        ]
75 Lu:      Are you tryin' to ignore
76          me, pretending that I'm not even
77          there?
78 KA, others: ((laugh))
            [            ]
79 Ph:              No, you are,
```

80		you are there. ((smiling broadly))
81	Na:	((laughs))
82	Ph:	An: the main reason — ((pointing to
		Lucille, addressing John))
83		*she* had a problem with Penny Cole
84		*and* Randy Roe!

In this exchange, Lucille overlaps the end of Phil's joking remarks to introduce what might be taken as joking itself, an attempt to be included in the risque label "sexy." Phil takes up her remark with a smile, but does not continue the joking by teasing her, as he might have done, about her sexiness or about her desire to "belong." Rather, he offers a strange proposition: Lucille is "there" because she had a problem with Randy and Penny.

Phil's remark looks like nonsense on its face, but it is easily understood as a reference, albeit somewhat awkwardly phrased, to a prior topic. Much earlier in Episode E, as I have mentioned, Lucille complained that "two people," whom she did not name, had been "taking out their anger" on her for something she did not do. It is a frequent although not obligatory Workshop practice to decline to name the persons one is accusing; other clients are invited to point the finger. At that point in the episode, John intervened to ask who these two people were, and Lucille, still not naming the cause of her problem herself, invited others to name them. The persons causing her problem were identified by John and Phil, with Lucille's confirmation, as Penny Cole and Randy Roe. After they were identified, though, John and Timmy took over the floor to discuss, in Episode F, *their* concerns about Penny and Randy. Lucille's problem was left hanging.

Thus in lines G:83-84, Phil is referring back to Lucille's vague problem. He might have made a smoother transition by saying something like, "No, Lucille, how could I ignore you? After all, you're another person, like John and Timmy, who has had trouble with Penny and Randy."

In referring to Lucille's prior topic, Phil can be seen as acknowledging that Lucille would like to get that topic back on the floor, and that her interjection, "Are you tryin' to ignore me?", is a move in that direction. (Lucille's second interruption a moment later, in lines G:135-140, provides stronger evidence that she would like to reintroduce her own problem.) However, while Phil reintroduces the topic for her by mentioning Penny and Randy, he does so in such a manner — addressing himself in dramatic tones to John — that the topic is taken out of her hands. John finds entree for taking up his own problem, already discussed in Episode F, regarding Penny and Randy (see transcript, lines F:86ff, in Appendix B). Phil supports John, and John goes on, beginning in line G:112, to "convert" to Phil's perception of Randy.

In the strange exchange between Lucille and Phil, then, I have argued that Lucille is seeking to open a place where she might regain the floor to discuss her own previously mentioned problem, while Phil is maneuvering to hold the floor himself. Keeping the floor was very important to Phil's goal. Up to this point he had accomplished a sound attack on John's friendship with Randy, but he had not yet won from John any sign of a renunciation of that friendship. If Lucille had relaunched a discussion of her own problems, Phil might not have had time to refocus on John before the end of the meeting.

Phil makes similar moves to hold the floor when Lucille seeks the floor in lines G:135-140 and lines G:160-161. In those instances, as in the one I have discussed, Lucille shows no indication that she intends to talk about Randy per se, even though she had earlier identified him as a cause of her problem. However, Phil brings Randy's name into it and steers the conversation back to his own concerns about Randy.

Of course, Lucille is not the only threat to Phil's possession of the floor. The transcript in Appendix B shows many attempts to take the floor, especially by Norman and Alan. However, Phil remains in control for many minutes. His humorous interludes, e.g., lines G:128-133, as well as his moments of high drama salted with taboo words, e.g., lines G:120-125, surely help him hold his audience against potential usurpers.

Providing a model. One technique for regulating another person's behavior is to provide a model for the other to copy. Teachers, for example, model speaking in full sentences for their students.[11]

Some of Phil's moves may be seen as providing a model for John's "conversion"; that is, they suggest the specific form which John's renunciation of Randy might take. In particular, Phil's statement in lines G:167-173 offers a model which John can copy almost directly: "Randy wants to get me in trouble." John does copy these words very closely, and thus signals the beginning of the narrative which marks his change of heart:

G:

167	Ph:	An' *I* think Randy Roe wants
168		to make up stories because s--*he*
169		wants to make me in trouble.
170		An' that's what he's

171   tryin' to do: get me
                [   ]
172 Jo: Uh, Philly?
173 Ph: in trouble.
174 Lu: (   )
                [   ]
175 Jo: Sometimes he got--
176   he got me in big trouble, too.

Phil had already brought up the theme that Randy would get John and Timmy in "trouble," in lines G:23-24 and lines G:45-46. However, for the first time, in the exchange excerpted above, he provides a model in the first person — and not by accident. I would argue that Phil deliberately makes the statement, "He wants to make me in trouble," as a model. It does not follow very strongly from what he has just been saying. The "stories" he says Randy makes are the stories, referred to above, that Randy and Sandra are cousins. While such "stories" do play an important role in determining who is on Randy's side,[12] it is not clear how Phil would get in "trouble" even if he publicly challenged Randy's alleged claim to be Sandra's cousin. However, it is a familiar Workshop format to say that someone "makes up stories" to "get me in trouble." The format makes an acceptable bridge from Phil's tirade about the cousins issue to his model of an anti-Randy statement, "He gets me in trouble."

3.4.4. *"Trouble"*

It is not surprising that Phil organized many of his moves toward "converting" John around the notion of "trouble." "Trouble" is a special and salient concept at the Workshop. Most clients want to avoid all kinds of "trouble" (Turner, Kernan, and Gelphman 1984), and to refer to someone as a "troublemaker" is a serious, fairly common accusation at the Workshop.

"Getting in trouble" refers to having a confrontation with an authority figure, whether a parent, foster parent, house parent, workshop counselor, or supervisor. The worst sanction clients can propose against someone who has been causing a problem is to "tell the counselor," thus getting the problematic person "in trouble."

As indicated in Table 2, a client occasionally admits getting himself "in trouble." More often, clients complain that someone else "got them in trouble." For instance, in the September 8 group meeting, Lucille lamented that "people page her to the office" (where the counselors are) for things she didn't do. Or on June 30, a female client confided to me and to other researchers that a male client" "got her in trouble" by falsely accusing her of hitting him. He had made the accusation to his counselor, who had apparently confronted the woman about it, and she was miserably anxious to clear her name.

Phil's allegation that Randy wants to get John and Timmy "in trouble," then, portrays Randy as the least desirable of companions.

3.4.5. *Steps in John's "conversion"*

I have mentioned only some of Phil's strategies in his successful effort to "convert" John. Now I will review the "conversion" briefly from John's perspective, to indicate the ways in which John participated actively rather than simply reacting to Phil's moves. This perception of John as an active participant will be important to the argument in the following section that John was pursuing his own private goals during this interaction.

John's change of heart takes the form, within Episode G, of an admission that Randy is not a nice person and has got John in "trouble." Given the weight of the concept of "trouble" at the Workshop, this admission was nearly enough by itself to sever John's alliance with Randy. However, John seemed to feel that some ambiguity in his position remained since he decided to make a further, unequivocal renunciation of Randy at the end of the meeting.

John's first negative statement about Randy occurs in lines G:112-117, when he announces that Randy sometimes acts "mean" to John's brother. However, signs of John's openness to the possibility of a "conversion" can be detected much earlier. John answered Phil's first two challenges of the form "Why you wanna go with [Randy]?", but on Phil's third round of the question, John passed up his opportunity to respond with a long silence (line G:40). Perhaps this silence simply meant that John had run out of replies to Phil's challenges, which he would continue to give if he could. However, it may also be read as a weakening of the will to fight back, a beginning of an admission that Phil is going to win the day.[13]

Seen in this light, it should not come entirely as a surprise when John volunteers his negative comment about Randy in lines G:112-117.[14] He takes the floor from Phil in lines G:103-104, announcing to Phil, "I have something else to say to you." John sidetracks himself when his attempt to address Phil in (mock?) formality by his last name misfires, but after repair by other clients he continues more seriously:

G:

112	Jo:	Randy Roe sometime act, uh
113		(pause)
114	Ph:	((smiling, pleased with self)) A
115		little kid.
116	Jo:	No, not a kid. *Mean*, still, like
117		he's — very — *meany* — to my brother;
118		Dennis Valerio's
119		my brother.

In this comment about Randy, John is "claiming" to agree with Phil's general perception that Randy is not nice. However, this claim does not put an end to the episode. Phil continues to berate Randy and to argue against Randy's alleged position in the "cousins" question. It would seem that John needs to make his point more strongly, and this he does in the narrative which concludes the episode. He does not "claim" but rather "displays" his agreement with Phil's position (that Randy gets people in trouble) by offering a story in which Randy got *him* in trouble (Sabsay, personal communication; Moerman, personal communication). Note that the "trouble" John got in was to be "bawled out" by his foster mother.

G:

175	Jo:	Sometimes he got —
176		he got me in big trouble, too.
177	Ph:	Keep away from him. For good.
178	Jo:	No, listen.
179	Ph:	An' I don't care
180		if he try to *kill* me.

      [   ]

181	Jo:	I know what he did.
182		I know what he did. He almost
183		killed my brother Dennis one
184		time.
185	Ph:	((smiling)) ( )
186		( ).

      [   ]

187	Jo:	He was getting very meany.
188		An' an' — he was (meaning) to, uh,
189		scratch his pants up.

191 Ph: That's a bad thing.
           [   ]
192 Jo: An', an' he blamed it
193   on me, because — it got blamed on
194   me, because when I went home that
195   day, my brother Dennis told my mom
196   that Randy Roe uh: scratched his
197   pants up.
198 Ph: Don't let him to do that again, make
199   your mother mad.
200 Jo: And my mom bawled me out.
201   That's all.

At this point, Phil lets John's narrative stand without further comment. Perhaps John's change of heart has indeed been demonstrated to his satisfaction. John, too, seems to treat the issue of taking sides against Randy as closed. After his, "That's all," in line G:201, he keeps the floor but clearly indicates that he is moving to a new topic: "And uh, excuse me, folks, but, uh, I wrote something *else* for Jenny." The researchers seem to consider the issue closed as well, for they let John go on for only a few remarks before interrupting him to give the floor to Norman, who has been angling for it for a long time.

Nonetheless, six minutes later, in the closing moments of the meeting, when many clients are already filing out, John raises the issue one more time. (See remarks by Schegloff and Sacks [1973] on the way unfinished business is likely to be raised during closings.) While Norman and Alan were presenting their problems to the group, John had apparently written one more note in his diary/notebook. He now asks to read it, and the researcher lets him do so amid the hubbub of side conversations and leave-taking. (See the full text of Episode L in Appendix B.)

From Episode L:
15 Jo: I — I am gonna make my own decision
16   about Randy Roe.
    .
    .
    .
19 Jo: I'm not gonna talk to him no more.
    .

21 Jo: An' I'm gonna be on Timmy's side.
22 No: That's ridiculous,
23   (   ).
                [   ]
24 Ti: All right, John.
               ((Shakes hands with John))
25 Jo: I'm goin' with you, not him.

In this episode, John makes a formal denunciation of Randy, addressed not to Phil, who seems not to be listening, but to the researcher, Jim Turner, and then to Timmy.

3.4.6. *Beneath the surface: Resolution of a conflict between John and Timmy?*

John's final renunciation of Randy contains a most puzzling element. In lines L:21 and L:25, John describes himself as making a choice between Randy and Timmy. He says he's going to be "on Timmy's side," not Randy's, as though Timmy and Randy had been on two different sides, and as though John had had to choose between them. The statement echoes lines 32-33 of Episode G, in which John says, "Laurie told me that she wants me to go with Randy Roe, not Timmy."

I will argue on the basis of this and other evidence that "what was going on" in Episode G involved more than simply Phil trying to regulate John's behavior. I believe there was a problem brewing between John and Timmy, and that John's change of heart about Randy resolved the problem so that John and Timmy could continue to be friends. To make this case I will have to refer not only to specific lines in Episode G and in Episode F which preceded it, but also to Workshop norms and concepts which have been uncovered in broader ethnographic research.

"*You have to take sides*." I have described the peer conflict discussed here in terms of "taking sides." There is, in fact, a Workshop norm that any client involved at all in the network cannot remain neutral. If A falls out with B, C cannot remain friends with both. Researchers have tried to challenge this position (for example, during the June 2 meeting) but clients hold to it as a given.

It follows that if John felt that he had to choose between Randy's side and Timmy's side, some kind of conflict must have existed between Timmy and Randy. Although Timmy claimed in line 10 of Episode G to be Randy's friend, it seems that John and Laurie did not accept his claim. That Tim himself doubted his friendship with Randy is suggested by Tim's silence throughout Episode G, when John faces Phil's attacks on Randy singlehandedly. Phil, too, seems to have taken Timmy's claim of friendship with Randy less seriously than John's claim, since he did not insist on any display of "conversion" by Timmy.[15] Close examination of Episode F suggests the possible source of conflict between Timmy and Randy.

"*Rumors*." Episode F begins with John reading a "speech" which Timmy had apparently dictated or at least outlined for him earlier in the day (Episode F, lines 24-36, in Appendix B). (Timmy often dictated "speeches" to John or to a researcher, presumably because his serious speech impediment made it difficult for him to hold the floor in meetings.) The "speech" is about "someone who's spreading rumors about Randy Roe," specifically spreading the "rumor" that Randy's parents are dead. In fact, Randy's parents *are* dead, and everyone at the Workshop already knows this. But by the special Workshop definition of "rumor," merely to pass information about a person behind his back — especially information about a taboo topic like death — is to spread a "rumor" (Turner, Kernan, and Gelphman 1984). One may infer from this passage that Randy believes someone has done him ill by spreading the "rumor" that his parents are dead.

"*Who did it*?" After John digresses regarding Penny Cole, Timmy interjects, "Who did it?" (Episode F, line 55). John makes a statement which implies that Penny was the person who spread the "rumors": "I don't know why Penny Cole said that to you about Randy's parents" (lines F:59-60). Then John backtracks to establish more clearly that Penny is the guilty party:

From Episode F:

70	Jo:	Is Penny Cole saying to you that
71		Randy's parents are dead?
		[ ]
72	Ti:	((gets mike, holds it low))
73	Ti:	Pe'y Cole said (to) Randy Roe.
74	Jo:	Penny Cole said it, right?
75	Ti:	Yes.
76		Not (me).
		[ ]
77	Jo:	O.K.

Timmy's "not me" in line F:76 suggests that someone may have accused him of spreading the "rumor." Given the evidence that Tim was on the outs with Randy, one may infer that Randy himself believed Tim to be the guilty party. Timmy seeks, with John's help, to place the blame on Penny instead. (John brings up the topic again in the middle of Episode G, lines 86-88, when he repeats the question, "An' why is Penny Cole, um:, making rumors about (Randy's parents)?")

Jim Turner has noted a tendency at the Workshop to respond to peer conflicts by blaming them on some blamable party. My data on Kinds of Problems and Kinds of Moves made in response to problem statements generally confirm the pattern discerned by Turner: when someone blames an absent or unrepresented party, the blame goes uncontested; when someone blames a person who is present, or the friend or ally of a person who is present, the blame is contested. John and Timmy knew that Penny Cole was an easily blamable party. No one in the group meeting would rise to defend her. Thus they could make the assertion without challenge that it was Penny rather than Timmy who had been spreading "rumors" behind Randy's back.

Final resolution. Although John entered the meeting in apparent alliance with his friend Timmy, then, their friendship was actually in jeopardy. Randy, I have argued, believed Timmy to have spread "rumors" about him and therefore considered Timmy his enemy, despite Timmy's protests to the contrary. John had clearly aligned himself with Randy, but by the rule that "you have to take sides," could not continue to be friends with Timmy and Randy at the same time. Thus Timmy and John's collaborative efforts in Episode F, while they seem on the surface to be a confused attempt to determine whether and why Penny spread "rumors" about their friend Randy, are actually an attempt to shift the blame for the "rumors" from Timmy to Penny. Their goal was to make it possible for Randy and Timmy to remain on the same side, and thus to save John from the need to choose between his two friends.

However, John's move toward reconciling Timmy with Randy was not at all certain of success. Phil's intervention, challenging John's friendship with Randy, offered a timely alternative solution to the crisis, namely, that John renounce Randy rather than attempt the reconciliation between Randy and Timmy. Whether Phil perceived his effort to "convert" John as leading ultimately to resolution of the crisis between John and Timmy is not clear from the transcript. It *is* clear from John's remarks in Episode L that John perceived his "conversion" as the end of his brewing conflict with Timmy.

3.4.7. *Summary*

What was going on in Episode G? In the context of a group counseling meeting in which clients of the sheltered workshop were encouraged to resolve peer problems among themselves, Phil raised the issue of "taking sides," a kind of peer problem unique to an identifiable group of clients in this meeting. He challenged John's friendship with a client who was not present, Randy, and made a series of moves which resulted in John's "conversion" from the pro-Randy to the anti-Randy camp. Phil's cognitive strategies included getting John to base his friendship with Randy on premises which could then be demolished, and restructuring John's perception of Randy's behavior. Phil's moves also required skill in social interaction, including the ability to mitigate his implied criticisms of John, and the ability to hold the floor by manipulating interruptions and by entertaining his "audience."

John displayed a gradual change of heart, beginning with mere silence in the face of Phil's challenge and ending, during the closing moments of the meeting, with an unequivocal renunciation of friendship with Randy. However, John's "conversion" during this meeting must be understood in the wider perspective of his weekly fluctuations from one side to the other in this continuing peer conflict. In fact, it was suggested that John's change of heart regarding Randy did not represent a true reversal in his perception of Randy as much as it represented a solution to a brewing conflict between John and his friend Timmy. It was argued on the basis of evidence from the conversation that Timmy, despite protests to the contrary, was in conflict with Randy and thus, by the rule that "you have to take sides," had been in danger of losing the friendship with John which both he and John valued.

3.5. Discussion

3.5.1. *Workshop norms and notions*

Throughout the analysis, I have explained parts of the transcript by referring to ways of doing things, standards for behavior, or concepts with which an outsider to Workshop Society would probably not be familiar. These techniques, notions, and norms (or recipes, beliefs, and rules, as Goodenough [1971] would call them) are part of the culture which clients at the Workshop share. At this point we do not yet know whether these cultural features developed only within this particular sheltered workshop in the course of interaction among its particular clients, or whether many of these features are common to other groups of retarded adults (by virtue either of similar socialization experiences or the similarity of the institutions in which they carry out their lives.)[16]

Some of the Workshop notions discussed in this paper point to important themes in the lives of the Workshop clients, and probably in the lives of most retarded adults. For example, behind the notion of "making up one's own mind" lie buried meanings about what it means to be an adult, which is a crucial problem for retarded persons. When they come of age, they are legally defined as adults, with such rights as voting and drinking; yet, in real life they find themselves dependent for jobs, homes, meals, and transportation on their parents, other caretakers, or social service personnel. Constantly in this ambiguous position, Workshop clients spend a lot of time affirming their adulthood, particularly during the group meetings. This seems to be why the word "baby" is such a strong insult at the Workshop, serving as a euphemism for the taboo word "retarded" (Turner, Kernan, and Gelphman 1984).

Similarly, clients act out in the concept of "getting in trouble" the childlike and dependent status they might deny if questioned directly. "Getting in trouble" usually refers to getting dressed down by one's counselor or, as in John's case, getting "bawled out" by one's foster mother — problems more likely to be associated with children and teenagers than with persons in their twenties, thirties, and forties.

While the identification of Workshop norms and notions is important in its own right, I have done it here to illuminate particular strategies clients used within one brief episode. For instance, I mentioned in passing Lucille's adherence to a Workshop tradition that the accuser not name the accused herself, and I showed how John and Phil took advantage of her culturally prescribed reticence to put into her mouth the names of persons *they* wanted to talk about. I also noted how Phil used the "I like you but —" strategy to good effect, and how he used words considered taboo in Workshop Society to titillate his audience and keep the floor.

More importantly, I have shown that cultural background is crucial to deciphering the meaning of whole stretches of discourse. Phil's moves toward "converting" John, for example, revolve around the Workshop notion of "getting in trouble." Understanding John's remarks requires considerably more ethnographic context. His question in lines G:86-88 about Penny Cole spreading "rumors," his mention in lines G:32-33 that Leslie wanted him to choose between Randy and Timmy, the final formulation of his denunciation of Randy in Episode L — these remain incoherent until the reader knows the Workshop tenets to which they refer. Only when you grasp the concept of "rumor" is it clear that Randy is upset over an injury. Only when you accept that clients "have to take sides" can you infer from John's need to choose between Randy and Timmy that Randy and Timmy are in conflict. Only when you understand the Workshop technique of resolving conflicts by blaming a blamable party do you see why Penny Cole's name comes up so often, and only then do you grasp the probable motivation behind much of John and Timmy's discourse.

Given the cultural background, the entire text of the transcript appears less bizarre and more rational. When the text appears more coherent, the speakers appear more intelligent. Thus the examination of Workshop culture becomes a tool for making better judgments about the competence of Workshop clients.

3.5.2. *The competence of retarded adults*

No one would claim that the clients studied here turned out, on close analysis, to be so competent that they no longer seem retarded. There are too many malapropisms, mispronunciations, and gaps in logical reasoning (e.g., Phil's argument in lines G:149-154 that cousins share the same last name) to make such a claim. However, the evidence in this paper does illustrate more, and more varied, competences than moderately retarded adults are often credited with.

First, as I have argued in the preceding section, once analysts grasp the cultural context, they are inclined to regard fewer of the retarded adults' statements as confused or illogical. True, clients may fail on many occasions to fill in important background information for their listeners—or at least for the listening researchers; it's not always clear to the researchers how much background knowledge other clients may be presumed to share. (See Sacks, Schegloff, and Jefferson 1974:727, on "recipient design"; cf. Sabsay and Kernan 1983.) Nonetheless, one becomes convinced that most of what the clients are saying makes sense to the speakers themselves, and that a good deal makes sense to the other clients they are addressing directly. John, Timmy, and probably Phil as well, followed Episode F significantly better than I did on my first hearing.

Secondly, I have shown that Phil demonstrated considerable skill at cognitive tasks like demolishing an oppponent's premises and restructuring others' perceptions. While clients vary in the degree to which they succeed at winning others to their point of view through argumentation, Phil is not the only client to experience some success. For instance, Hal's skill at maneuvering fellow clients to solutions has been documented in Turner (1983) and Turner, Kernan, and Gelphman (1984). Even John, while more often "influenced" by others, succeeded in "converting" Phil to Randy's side in June 2 meeting. In a later paper I hope to compare Phil's successes and failures with those of other clients to better understand the range of argumentative and persuasive skills on which clients draw, and to identify the situations in which those kinds of skills are most likely to work.

Thirdly, I have documented Phil's interactional competence, including communicative skills like holding the floor through drama and humor, and the cognitive and social skills required to regulate others' behavior. Again, clients vary widely in their communicative and interactional competence. Some, like Timmy, have difficulty simply pronouncing words clearly enough to be understood; others, like Norman, speak clearly but rely on researchers' intervention to gain the floor. However, while Phil may represent the higher end of the scale in communicative skills at the workshop, he is not alone among the mildly and moderately retarded clients who can manage a conversation with some finesse.

If this case study and future comparative studies do reveal greater and more varied competence among retarded adults than is generally assumed, how is this so? In part, credit goes to the method of analysis. Only such detailed analysis of conversations among retarded adults, informed by such rich ethnographic information, could have pointed out the intricate social and cognitive operations of which the adults are capable. Few such studies have been done (although see Price-Williams and Sabsay [1979] for a related study of the profoundly retarded).

More fundamentally, conversations such as the one examined here have to exist before they can be studied. As suggested by the neo-Vygotskian literature cited in the Introduction, the skills people exhibit depend on the "activity" in which they exhibit them, and the "activity" described in this paper is unusual. First, there had to be this sheltered workshop itself, in which a social life is allowed to flourish among a large group of retarded adults. Then there had to be the formation of the group meeting as an "activity" in which Workshop clients come with their own agenda and attempt to resolve conflicts themselves. Furthermore, the group meeting had to be structured in such a way that clients could learn the social and cognitive skills of peer problem resolution, gradually depending less and less on regulation by more capable others. Finally, the context of the particular meeting studied had to foster the use of clients' developing skills; as I have hinted, in other meetings when the problem, or Phil's emotional involvement with it, or the researchers' role varied, Phil did not always demonstrate the same level of skill.

In other words, the skills displayed by Phil and other clients in the group meetings might never have developed in another setting. Moreover, it is not yet known to what extent clients "internalize" the skills they have learned to use within the group meetings. The group meetings could conceivably be the kind of situation which Hood, McDermott, and Cole (1980: 158) describe, in which people achieve what they achieve *only* through constant mutual regulation. Without regulation by researchers, or by peers who had shared the group meeting experience, would a client be able to transfer his competence at holding the floor, persuading, arguing, mitigating criticism, and the like to other situations? Would it be fair to expect that a researcher could test the competences developed in group meetings by the usual standardized techniques?

Ultimately, we will have to answer these questions because of their practical implications. Administrators of other sheltered workshops, for instance, may decide whether to invest resources in conducting group counseling sessions for clients on the basis of the "transferability" of skills acquired in those sessions. But for the researchers currently running the group meetings at the Workshop, the question is not burning. They know already that they have structured one hour per week, if not more, in which a number of Workshop clients can conduct their affairs with greater autonomy and dignity.

4. DISPLAYING COMPETENCE: PEER INTERACTION IN A GROUP HOME FOR RETARDED ADULTS

Martha Platt

4.1. Introduction

The speech of mentally retarded individuals has largely been viewed in terms of deficits in articulation and grammar (e.g., Schiefelbusch 1972). This concern with linguistic competence is, in fact, sometimes reflected in the conversations of retarded speakers themselves. The six retarded women whose communicative abilities are the focus of the present study evidenced their awareness that the grammatical form of their own and others' speech could be interpreted as an index of competence (cf. Turner, Kernan, and Gelphman 1984). Aspects of pronunciation and lexical choice were the most common sources of comment, both because of perceived deviance from, and conformity with, grammatical norms. For example, speakers commented on the pronunciation of potentially tongue-tripping words such as "psychologist" or "marinated cucumbers," or on the use of the word "salad" to refer to a bowl of cabbage.

Like many retarded persons, these women participate in regular sessions with a speech therapist, whose primary job is to mitigate the articulation and grammatical deficits in her clients' speech. It hardly seems surprising that these retarded individuals would internalize the values and emphasis implicit in the speech therapy program.

This is not to say that the goals of the speech therapist or of traditional language research concerning mentally retarded individuals should be abandoned. However, it is important to recognize that this perspective severely constrains the way in which language use in this population is viewed and evaluated. Two major problems with the focus on grammatical deficits are: (1) that it encourages a view of retarded persons' speech in which language use remains constant across time and space, and (2) that it emphasizes the intra-psychological aspect of language use to the detriment of interpsychological processes. That is, this perspective treats the language deficits observed in these individuals' speech as a unitary set of characteristics that have the same potential for precipitating communicative distress in all social settings, and further, perpetuates the idea that these deficits cannot be mitigated by co-participants in these settings.

However, recent research has demonstrated that retarded speakers are sensitive not only to linguistic form but also to its appropriateness relative to a particular social setting (e.g., Anderson-Levitt this volume; Bedrosian and Prutting 1978; Owings and McManus 1980). This research derives from an approach which treats language use as a reflection of more general norms for social interaction within a particular culture (or subculture) (e.g., Hymes 1972). Such contextual variables as the social identities of speakers (e.g., adults labelled mentally retarded), the setting in which speech takes place (e.g., a group home for retarded adults) and the goals speakers pursue through their use of language (e.g., displaying knowledge about household routines) are all factors that may influence the formal properties of language as it is used in a particular situation. The concern with speakers' understanding of the social as well as grammatical underpinnings of language involves an examination of speakers' (e.g., retarded adults') understanding of how a linguistic system is used to convey social information.

An important methodological implication of the theoretical approach outlined above is a reliance on spontaneous speech collected in naturalistic settings. Since the study of communicative competence entails an assessment of what speakers really do with language in a variety of culturally meaningful situations, it is essential to collect data in such a way as to capture this behavior (cf. discussion of "ecological validity," Cole, Hood, and McDermott 1982; Schieffelin 1979). The present study, informed by this perspective, will draw primarily on such data.

4.2. Objectives

The purpose of this study is to assess conversational interaction among retarded adults in terms of the social setting in which it takes place. Specifically, this report examines spontaneous verbal interaction in a group home for six mildly and moderately retarded women. Three principal features of the social setting are addressed: (1) the major goals of the group home as perceived and pursued by residents and staff; (2) the verbal strategies used by residents for achieving these goals; and (3) some conversational consequences of these strategies.

4.3. Data base and methodology

The analysis presented here is based on audio-recordings of naturally occurring conversations between six mildly and moderately retarded women and the resident care provider. In some instances, the researcher also participated in conversation; however, the bulk of conversational interaction recorded took place between residents or between residents and the care provider. Before any recordings were made, the home was visited weekly for four consecutive weeks in the late afternoon and early evening, including dinner. These initial visits established rapport with residents and allowed for the collection of observational data on both verbal and nonverbal behavior. On the fifth visit, the tape recorder was turned on at dinnertime, including the periods before and after when kitchen chores related to meal preparation and clean-up were being performed. Three dinnertime recordings were made in this way, for a total of approximately 90 minutes.

Each recording was initially transcribed by the author using transcription conventions outlined in Sacks, Schegloff, and Jefferson (1974) and elaborated in Ochs (1979). Following this, the transcript was verified by the resident care provider, trained in the transcription conventions referred to above. The care provider was instructed to fill in unclear utterances, check the identity of speakers, and note any other disagreements with the material set down in the initial transcription. Upon completion of this second phase, the transcript was again checked by the author. In most cases, the care provider's transcription was judged to be accurate. However, in cases in which the author's transcription continued to differ from that of the care provider, both transcriptions were included, indicating that no agreement was reached.

The transcribed conversational data are supplemented by fieldnotes taken after each visit. The notes span weekly visits over a five-month period, as well as two weekend visits, one at the group home, the other on a three-day trip.

4.4. The setting

4.4.1. *Physical characteristics*

The four-bedroom residential facility visited for this study opened in August 1981. It provides three bedrooms, each shared by two residents, with a fourth room for the care provider. A large living room and kitchen complete the layout. This home is one of four, identical in size and layout, which form a square around a large grassy courtyard. All four facilities are quite comfortable and homelike.

4.4.2. *Residents*

The six female residents of the group home range in age from 28 to 43, with I.Q.'s ranging from 54 to 80.[17] All seem to have comparable abilities in day-to-day household and self-maintenance tasks, with the exception of the most recently arrived resident, Nancy, who appears markedly less competent in these areas. Four of the women, Grace, Nancy, Joanne and Carol, work at a sheltered workshop across the street from their home (the workshop described in Anderson-Levitt, this volume; Graffam, this volume; Graffam and Turner 1984; Turner 1983). The other two women spend their days in a different setting. Marcy works at a local fast food restaurant five days a week (part time), while Elaine attends special classes at a nearby junior college. The care provider is a woman in her mid-twenties who is pursuing a degree in special education.

4.4.3. *Goals of the group home*

Like their nonretarded counterparts, the behavior of mentally retarded persons is constrained by the social structure of the settings in which they participate. However, unlike nonretarded persons, adults labeled retarded have a history of incompetence, on the basis of which a variety of generalized expectations and particular social settings have been constructed. One such setting is the small board and care facility, or group home, such as the one visited for this study. The goals of the group home, as stated in its charter, are "to make available to the developmentally disabled those patterns, conditions, situations, opportunities and responsibilities of everyday life" and "to provide an environment which will facilitate increased social functioning of … residents. The major areas of training emphasis will be those of self-help, communication, socialization and recreation skills." This prescriptive statement is reflected in the views of both residents and care provider. These individuals see the group home as a place for retarded residents to learn how to master the practical skills required for day-to-day living. In general, the emphasis is on being able to master the complex of details which make up one's day-to-day existence. In this particular house, residents are expected to take responsibility for household chores according to a prearranged schedule and to keep track of who does what each day. Other daily life skills, including banking, budgeting, and shopping for personal items are areas in which residents have the opportunity to learn and practice everyday skills. Thus, an important goal of the group home, recognized by residents and care provider, is to assist residents in achieving competence in everyday living skills.

As a result, residents are somewhat preoccupied with displaying their competence in these areas. Specifically, these women often focus attention on their own and others' competence in displaying utilitarian knowledge. They are particularly concerned with co-residents' ability to remember items of information and recount them accurately, perform household tasks, maintain personal appearance, and speak clearly.

Attention is similarly drawn to incompetence in these areas. This is particularly true because the inability or unwillingness of one household member to effectively perform tasks or display knowledge is felt by the entire household in very tangible ways. When Nancy overloaded the washing machine, for example, causing it to break down, everyone was inconvenienced. Another aspect of behavior that affects all household members is noncompliance. When, for example, a resident fails to perform her assigned household task, others must decide how to resolve the situation (e.g., do it themselves, tell the care provider, badger the non-compliant resident). This problem could, of course, occur in any group living situation, but in this case it takes on greater urgency because of licensing regulations. Board and care facilities such as this one are subject to unannounced visits by health inspectors.

In addition to talk about task performance, much conversation centers on the particulars of orchestrating many schedules and activities so as to minimize conflict. Times and dates are often focal points of these discussions. The community calendar in the kitchen, on which clients write down appointments, meetings, etc. testifies to the concern for integrating everyone's schedules as harmoniously as possible. Although, again, this could be a central concern in any group living situation, it takes on an even greater salience here because of residents' relative lack of independence. For example, only the care provider drives and has a key to the apartment, and residents are not allowed to be at home without the care provider. Hence, all arrangements, whether for domestic or outside activities, must be scheduled with these basic constraints in mind.

This points out the contradictory messages conveyed to retarded adults in this situation. On the one hand, residents are provided with opportunities to acquire and improve everyday life skills and to develop social relationships, with an eye towards fostering independence and autonomy. On the other hand, their ability to exercise individual preference and decision-making power may be restricted by the demands of the group living situation and their identification as "less-than-fully-competent."

The social organization and character of conversational interaction in the group home stand in contrast to these same features of another important social setting in the lives of mentally retarded adults — a sheltered workshop. Four of the six group home residents spend the working day at such a facility located across the street from their home (see Turner [1983] for a detailed description of the physical and social characteristics of this workshop). Unlike the group home, "the workshop provides, for most of its members, the principal setting in which they engage in social interaction, talk, form friendships and in general, live their daily lives" (Turner, Kernan, and Gelphman 1984: 44). In this setting, interaction is in general guided by an "implicit social contract" in which maintaining social harmony and an egalitarian social structure take precedence over the establishment of objective truth and the assertion or display of relatively superior individual competence. (See Turner [1983] and Turner, Kernan, and Gelphman [1984] for further discussion of social interaction in the sheltered workshop.)

Residents of the group home, on the other hand, are not a close-knit social group. Their primary social relationships are with individuals outside this setting. Indeed, there is little "talk-for-the-sake-of-talk" in this context as there is in the workshop. Instead, residents tend to spend much of their time at home in their own rooms when not engaged in household activities requiring group participation. In contrast to the sheltered workshop, interaction in the group home often focuses on the establishment of objective truth and the assertion of individual competence, frequently at the expense of social harmony.

4.4.4. *Dinner preparation*

Since the analysis presented here is based on recordings of dinnertime conversation, a brief description of the household routines associated with this activity will help set the stage for the discussion of conversational patterns. Dinner is often prepared by one or more of the residents, usually with some degree of assistance from the care provider. Several of the women have participated in cooking classes and enjoy trying out new recipes; this is encouraged by the care provider. In addition to tasks involved in food preparation, residents also take responsibility for setting the table and for clearing it and washing the dishes after the meal.

The actual amount of time residents sit at the dinner table is relatively short. There is no extended period of time after eating in which people remain seated at the table and engage in conversation. For the most part, when residents finish eating they take their plate to the sink and either leave the room to attend to other matters or remain in the kitchen to begin clean-up chores. Thus, while the slower women are still eating, others might be doing the dishes or watching television. It should be noted that since the cooking and eating areas are contiguous, verbal exchanges can easily take place (and often do) between persons still seated at the table and those engaged in clean-up tasks.

4.5. A situated definition of competence

So far, this report has described the primary goals of the group home, goals designed to develop residents' daily living skills. This section concerns the way in which residents use this aspect of the social structure of the group home to define and assess their own and others' competence. The social features of the group home setting define certain achievements necessary for residents to claim status as competent household members. For the six residents of this group home, competence means being able to display the utilitarian knowledge and abilities pertaining to everyday life on which the residential training program focuses. This can be seen in self-descriptions provided by residents of group homes (J. Turner, personal communication). The following excerpt is taken from the self-description of a female resident of another group home. It is in response to the very general question "Can you tell me about yourself?" or "What kind of person are you?"

> I do work around the house. Run the vacuum in the house. I run the vacuum in my room. I clean the mirrors in the bathroom....

Retarded and nonretarded persons alike seek to present themselves as competent relative to the requirements or expectations operating in the social situation in which they are participating. When considering the behavior of retarded adults in a group home, this emphasis on the influence of social context on self-presentation allows for an account of these individuals' behavior which shows their sensitivity to the constraints impinging upon their lives as group home residents.

Retarded individuals' concern with appearing competent has been documented in a variety of ethnographic studies. Edgerton (1967) portrayed the lengths to which retarded persons go to sustain a facade of normalcy and competency for others ignorant of the stigmatizing characteristic attributed to them. Turner (1983) and Turner, Kernan, and, Gelphman (1984) have shown that clients at a sheltered workshop are similarly concerned with presenting themselves as competent adults leading normal lives. Many individuals engage in "normalcy fabrication," in which they attempt to present themselves "as leading a less restricted and more 'normal' life than he or she actually does" (Turner, Kernan, and Gelphman 1984: 45). There has evolved "an implicit social contract … that produces the rule of etiquette which dictates that members should be allowed to maintain their dignity by presenting a demeanor of competency" (Turner, Kernan, and Gelphman 1984: 42). Most workshop members abide by this rule. They avoid potentially face-threatening topics and refrain from challenging the competency claims of others. Graffam (this volume) also documents that competence is a major recurring issue in peer counseling sessions for retarded adults at the same workshop. This concern with one's own and others' competence is of primary importance to group home residents as well. Several of them have recounted experiences to the researcher in which their ability to perform in a competitive employment or independent living situation was challenged. By continually asserting their competence to perform in a situation created with their particular needs in mind, residents are able to transcend to some extent these stigmatizing experiences.

One of the recurring conversational topics reflecting residents' concerns with competence is that involving the weekly scheduling of household duties. The care provider in this home has made it clear that she expects residents to take total responsibility for the scheduling and completion of household chores. Every Sunday residents decide on the schedule for the coming week; however, the outcome of this process is not recorded in written form. Hence, throughout the week there is continual debate and negotiation between residents and between residents and the care provider as to who agreed to do what. In addition, discussion occurs when changes in the schedule must be made due to unforeseen outside commitments of household members. Residents use these conversational transactions as opportunities to display their ability to keep track of those items of information relating to at least their own, and often others', role in the larger network of information and responsibilities. The salience and frequency of this topic in the conversations of group home residents cannot be overemphasized. Performing household chores correctly, with dispatch and according to schedule, is a major way in which residents may claim status as competent adults in this setting.

These exchanges typically begin with an announcement by one of the residents regarding her role in the task schedule. Other residents respond by announcing their own roles in a parallel display of mundane knowledge. They also respond by challenging the factual accuracy of an announcement made by another speaker, using the perceived error of the other speaker as a foil for displaying their own competence. These exchanges thus sometimes take on a competetive air. (This observation on the quality of conversational interaction in a group home has been corroborated for a similar home for four female residents located in a different city [Kristina Kennann, personal communication].)

The following is an example of one such discussion:[18]

EXAMPLE 1 (12-8-83):

1	Grace:	Oh good ..only got two things to do tonight.
2	Marcy:	Yeah I know, so do I.
3	Grace:	The shower and my bed- m- I dust yesterday.
4	Marcy:	I wash Tuesday.
5	Joanne:	I got //two.]
	[	
6	Marcy:	//(I wanna do the entry floor).]
7	Joanne:	This- bathtub and the floor that's all.
8	Grace:	No Nancy doing the floor in here.
9	Nancy:	Oh yeah.
10	Joanne:	Not uh- in my //bathroom that's all.]
	[	
11	Grace:	//I know that] ((pause)) I- I d- I do- Nancy, she's right..you do the entry.
12	Nancy:	Oh I see.

In line 1 Grace announces her chores for that evening. This is the third time in the transcript that she makes this announcement, but the first time that it is responded to, in this case by Marcy in line 2. In lines 3 and 4, Grace and Marcy exchange information about their specific tasks for that day (Tuesday). Joanne enters the conversation in lines 5 and 7 with her own announcement. She is challenged by Grace in line 8, who misinterprets Joanne's mention of "the floor" as being the kitchen floor. Joanne clarifies in line 10 that it is the bathroom floor she is talking about. Grace's response in line 11 asserts her knowledge of Joanne's responsibilities and repeats from line 8 her display of knowledge about Nancy's role. Throughout this exchange, Grace, Marcy, and Joanne have used their turns at talk to demonstrate to one another that they keep track of their own — and other residents' — household respon-

sibilities. Only Nancy, the least competent resident, has merely responded to
the other residents' displays rather than providing her own.

4.6. Verbal strategies for displaying competence

One of the overriding social functions of language, that of both retarded
and nonretarded speakers, is to assert the speaker's status as a competent
member of society. As Example 1 illustrates, residents use language to display
their competence in the areas deemed important for their group living situation. This display often takes the form of announcing facts about their daily
lives, challenging the accuracy of others' statements, and negotiating solutions to practical problems associated with household management (e.g.,
whose turn it is to do the dishes).

A pervasive characteristic of verbal interaction in the group home is residents' pronounced tendency to use language to lay personal claim to items of
information, regardless of whether the information has already been contributed by a co-participant in the conversation. Residents often assert their
competence by using their turns at talk to contribute items of information
related to household routines and other daily life events. Conversational
interaction characterized by interlocutors constantly contributing information that is already shared by co-participants violates a basic conversational
"maxim" (Grice 1975), namely, that speakers should not use their turn at talk
to provide listeners with information they already know. However, for group
home residents, this cross-situational constraint on conversation appears to
be superceded by the organization of interaction in this particular setting.
That is, the display of competence vis-a-vis the social goals inherent in the
group home setting takes precedence over more general conversational rules
concerning shared information.

One of the most striking features of residents' discourse is the pervasive
use of the response "I know," when a less explicit backchannel acknowledgement by the listener (e.g., "yeah," "okay," or "mm-hm") would be more
appropriate. A typical interchange along these lines involves a speaker making an announcement concerning the everyday maintenance and communal
activities of the household and one or more listeners asserting their prior
knowledge of the information in question. Such an exchange is presented
below:

EXAMPLE 2 (11-8-83): This conversation took place on a Tuesday. It
had rained the previous Tuesday, but was fair on this day.

1	Grace:	Last week Tues- last Tuesday's raining not this Tuesday not raining.
2	Marcy:	I know ((pause)) //It was nice.]
	[	
3	Elaine:	//It sure was nice out today.]
4	Marcy:	It was nice.
5	Carol:	I know last Tuesday was rainin', //I *know*.]
	[	
6	Elaine:	//Who] else needs ice?

In this example, Grace introduces the topic of the weather that day compared to the Tuesday before (line 1). Marcy and Elaine respond to this contribution with an elaboration of the topic (lines 2-4). In line 2, Marcy's comment on the weather is preceded by an acknowledgement, "I know." Although this response serves the function of acknowledgement of, and agreement with, the prior speaker's utterance, it does so more explicitly than is appropriate. That is, in addition to functioning as a marker of acknowledgement of agreement, it also explicitly indicates *prior knowledge* of the information contained in Grace's utterance. Carol's turn at talk (line 5) treats Grace's utterance not so much as a topic initiating statement, but rather as simply a piece of information about which she can assert her prior knowledge. This exchange illustrates that, for Carol at least, topic-initiations contributed by her interlocutors provide an oppportunity for display of knowledge about that information contained in the prior turn, not for elaboration of the content of the topic-initiating turn.

EXAMPLE 3 (12-8-83):

1	Marcy:	Hey Elaine, are we gonna stop at- at Barstow on our way up?
2	Elaine:	Yes.
3	Marcy:	Well?
4	Grace:·	Yes //Barstow.]
	[	
5	Joanne:	//Barstow.]
6	Grace:	Me and Carol and- and my sister have m- my do- my- dollar tificates* [=certificates]
7	Marcy:	I know that.
8	Joanne:	I know that.

* discount coupons for MacDonald's hamburgers

In example 3, lines 7 and 8, both Marcy and Joanne use the response "I know" in a similar manner to Carol in example 2. In lines 1 to 5, it is established that the bus taking residents to Lås Vegas for the weekend will stop at Barstow for lunch. In line 6, Grace comments on the fact that she and others have discount coupons which she wants to use in Barstow. Rather than elaborating on Grace's assertion, both Marcy and Joanne simply claim prior knowledge of this information. Again, in this example, speakers appear to use prior turns of others as an opportunity to display prior knowledge of the content of this turn, rather than contribute new information.

These two examples illustrate a major feature of peer conversation in this setting: the preference for explicitly asserting prior knowledge of information contributed by another speaker either instead of or in combination with contributing new topic-relevant information.

Examples 2 and 3 showed the manner in which residents assert prior knowledge of information contributed by their interlocutors. There are, in addition, many instances in which residents seek to display their knowledge of the topic at hand. As example 4 illustrates, this conversational behavior often generates a sequence of overlapped turns. In some instances, a speaker provides the same information as another, i.e., "chimes in"; in other cases, overlap occurs when speakers simultaneously collaborate on a topic by contributing different items of information.

EXAMPLE 4 (11-8-83): Residents are discussing whether Nancy's mother will be going with them on a weekend trip to Las Vegas. Nancy's mother is not liked by other residents. (Susan is the resident care provider.)

1	Susan:	Um. Nancy, is your mom going to Vegas?
	((pause))	
2	Susan:	Is she? Is your mom going to Las Vegas?
3	Nancy:	//I don't know.]
	[	
4	Carol:	//Oh boy I hope not.]
5	Marcy:	*Carol*, that isn't nice=
6	Susan:	=Shh
7	Nancy:	She- she- she doesn't know when it is.
	((pause))	
8	Susan:	((irritated)) The Las Vegas trip that she went on last year.

9	Grace:	Yeah d-
10	Joanne:	Yeah.
11	Elaine:	It's December ninth, tenth //and eleventh.]
	[	
12	Marcy:	//and eleventh.]
13	Nancy:	In December?
14	Elaine:	//Yeah.]
	[	
15	Marcy:	//Yeah.]
16	Elaine:	Doesn't your //mom] get a bulletin?
	[	
17	Grace:	//Yeah.]
18	Elaine:	Up there? ((points to bulletin posted on kitchen bulletin board))
19	Nancy:	You mean this kind?
20	Elaine:	Yeah, doesn't your mom get a bulletin?
21	Marcy:	//I hope not.]
	[	
22	Joanne:	//( )]
23	Nancy:	I don't think she- I don't- I don't think she has one or not.
24	Elaine:	My dad sends one out //every month.]
	[	
25	Marcy:	//to every parent] to every parent.
26	Susan:	You know what? We'll have to ask your mom on Sunday to find out if //she's going.]
	[	
27	Joanne:	//forget it.]
28	Nancy:	Yeah, I think you better.
29	Susan:	Or *you* can ask her.
30	Joanne:	Yeah.
31	Susan:	On Sunday.
32	Grace:	Yeah.

This exchange shows residents' response to Nancy's incompetence, i.e., her inability to keep track of the details involved in a household activity, in this case, the annual Las Vegas trip. All speakers display their knowledge concerning the trip in some way, from simply using an agreement marker, "yeah," as in lines 14-15 and 17, to contributing a specific item of information,

as in lines 11-12 and 24-25. In each instance, these displays are either partially
or completely simultaneous.

Another manifestation of residents' use of language to display their competence is presented in example 5.

EXAMPLE 5 (11-8-83)

1   Elaine: Well *ask* Nancy, don't look ((N is looking at bowl of
                    cabbage))
2   Nancy: Salad please.
3   Elaine: That's not salad.
4   Joanne: It's cabbage.
5   Nancy: Cabbage?=
6   Grace: //Cabbage.]
       [
7   Elaine   //Cabbage.]

This exchange demonstrates how display of knowledge takes precedence
over an appropriate response to the intent of a speaker's utterance. In line 1,
Elaine admonishes Nancy to be explicit about what it is she wants. This utterance makes it clear that Elaine has followed Nancy's gaze and can therefore
identify the object which Nancy requests in line 2. However, rather than
responding to Nancy's request using the contextual cues provided by gaze
direction, Elaine and then also Joanne and Grace make their responses con-
tingent on Nancy's incorrect lexical choice. Following this exchange, Elaine
still did not pass the cabbage to Nancy, but instead, served her from the bowl
herself.

Residents' verbal reaction to Nancy's incompetence can be seen in
examples 4 and 5 above. In these cases, Nancy's apparent inability to keep
track of details relating to household activities or, as in example 5, to properly
identify familiar objects, generates knowledge displays on the part of other
residents. This response to apparent incompetence is not limited to Nancy's
contributions to conversational interaction, as example 6 shows.

EXAMPLE 6 (11-8-83): Residents are discussing the fact that Marcy has
apparently forgotten about Phil's (a resident of another group home)
vacation plans, announced at the previous Tuesday night residents'
meeting. Prior to line 1, residents have responded to Marcy's question
about whether Phil will be at work the following day.

1   Carol: He's on vacation.
2   Marcy: Oh, oh okay.

3	Carol:	He's on vacation.
4	Marcy:	Well I didn't know that.
5	Grace:	//Yeah.]
	[	
6	Elaine:	//But] he's gonna go on the next night uh-
7	Carol:	The sixteenth mm=
8	Elaine:	=Uh okay.
9	Carol:	He's on vacation ( ) didn't he tell- didn't he tell you that go on vacation?
10	Grace:	Yeah, //I..did.]
	[	
11	Marcy:	//Yeah, yeah, yeah] yeah I forgot //about that.]
	[	
12	Carol:	//He mentioned] it last Tuesday in the meeting.
13	Marcy:	I forgot=
14	Carol:	=Wake up.
15	Marcy:	I'm half as//leep.]
	[	
16	Grace:	//Susan?]
	[	
17	Carol:	//Didn't] he men- he mentioned it last Tuesday in the meeting, didn't he mention it last week?
18	Grace:	Yes.
19	Carol:	He told Elaine.
20	Elaine:	Yeah.
21	Carol:	See? Elaine didn't forget.
22	Marcy:	Okay.
23	Carol:	Marcy forgot.
24	Grace:	Yeah.

In this prolonged exchange, Carol uses Marcy's apparent lack of knowledge as a foil for displaying her own knowledge of the topic at hand, i.e., Phil's vacation plans. Carol asserts the critical information concerning Phil three times, in lines 1, 3 and 9. Marcy's response to these assertions becomes progressively more revealing as to the state of her knowledge of this information: "oh, oh okay" (line 2), "well, I didn't know that" (line 4), "yeah I forgot about that" (line 11). From lines 17 to 20, Carol solicits confirmation of her assertion from other residents. She then uses Elaine's response in line 20 as further means to emphasize Marcy's perceived incompetence. Finally, in lines 23 and 24, Carol and Grace collaborate in reiterating the nature of Marcy's shortcoming. This example once again illustrates the way in which residents use the perceived incompetence of one household member as a foil for displaying their own knowledge of the information in question.

In many instances, conversational interaction consists of one or more speakers challenging information contributed by another speaker. These cases most often focus on details of time and place or other minutiae of residents' day-to-day existence.

EXAMPLE 7 (10-11-83): Carol and Grace are discussing the schedule of household tasks. Every Sunday, residents figure out who is responsible for what tasks during the coming week.

1	Grace:	I do my- the dishes on the twenty-fourth.
	((pause))	
2	Grace:	I do the dishes on the twenty-fourth.
3	Carol:	What do you mean the twenty-fourth?
4	Grace:	Monday.
5	Carol:	Who's gonna do it this Monday the *seventeenth* when we change on Sunday?
6	Grace:	I said the twenty-fourth.
7	Carol:	Well, I'm not doin' it, I did it already.

In this example, both Carol and Grace display their knowledge of household routines in the context of negotiating the weekly task schedule. In line 1, Grace announces her task responsibility for two weeks following, and repeats this announcement in line 2. Carol challenges this assertion with a question in line 3. Grace's response in line 4 does not address the intent of Carol's question (i.e., what about next week?), rather, she uses her turn at talk to further display her knowledge about the details of her role in the schedule of tasks. In line 5, Carol makes the intent of her question in line 3 explicit. Grace, instead of admitting that she doesn't know, uses her turn to display the knowledge she does have by repeating her prior contribution. Finally, in line 7, Carol displays knowledge of her role in the task schedule.

EXAMPLE 8 (10-11-83): Residents are discussing the accuracy of Phil's statement concerning the time of his arrival at work.

1	Grace:	What time you came to work?
2	Phil:	Ten ten, late.
3	Carol:	((loud)) Ten *after* ...eleven.
4	Phil:	Ten ten.

5	Carol:	I looked at my watch, it was ten after eleven.
6	Phil:	Uh, you're wacky.
7	Carol:	No, it was almost lunchtime.
8	Joanne:	Yes, Phil.
9	Carol:	(Don't call me wacky.)
10	Phil:	//It was ten after ten.
		[
11	?:	//I don't like that 'bout Carol.]
12	Joanne:	I saw you coming //in.]
		[
13	Carol:	//He] came back ten to twelve.*
14	Grace:	Yeah, ten to twelve.
		((pause))
15	Phil:	((defensively)) I said I wake up at ten ten.
16	Carol:	You wake up at ten ten=
17	Phil:	=Look Carol, stop.
18	Carol:	You wake up at ten minutes to //to eleven.]
		[
19	Phil:	//Alright, Carol], don't be ( ).
20	Carol:	I think it's ten minutes to //eleven.]
		[
21	Grace:	//I came] *back* at ten to twelve.**
22	Carol:	Ten to twelve?
23	Grace:	Yeah.
24	Phil:	//Who did?]
		[
25	Carol:	///I know-] she did..ate lunch at ten to twelve.

*   came back home from work
** came back home from an appointment

Example 8 presents another instance in which the accuracy of a speaker's statement is challenged. In this case, several residents collaborate in challenging Phil's assertion about when he arrived at work. Lines 1 and 2, Grace's question and Phil's response, toether function as an announcement of the time of Phil's arrival at work. From lines 3 to 6, Carol challenges Phil, who maintains his position. In line 8, Joanne enters the conversation confirming Carol's challenge to Phil. She elaborates in line 12. Grace then rejoins the conversation in line 14, confirming Carol's assertion as to when Phil returned home. In line 15, after a pause of several seconds, Phil claims that his original assertion concerned the time he woke up. Carol continues to challenge this in lines 18 and 20. Grace then contributes information about her own schedule in line 21, apparently building on Carol's claim in line 13. Carol queries this assertion in line 22 and Grace confirms it. Then finally in line 25, Carol responds with "I know," asserting prior knowledge of the information contributed by Grace (cf. examples 2 and 3). Thus, Carol uses announcements by both Phil and Grace to display her knowledge of temporal information. Joanne and Grace similarly use their turns at talk to display knowledge.

4.7. Summary

The purpose of this overview of conversational interaction among moderately and mildly mentally retarded adults has been to show the relationship between social setting and language use in this population. This account has emphasized the "normalizing" character of the goals prescribed for residents of the group home. These goals, which include the unassisted exercise of everyday living skills, particularly as they relate to household maintenance and scheduling of activities, center on the development of normal, adult competence. However, these goals are pursued in a context in which residents' adult status is compromised. That is, residents are not only subject to restrictions arising from their "less-than-adult" status, but the very training and experience provided for them is predicated on the assumption that they are not competent, and hence, not fully adult.

Further, this study has outlined certain verbal strategies of residents that reflect these two conflicting social features of the group home setting. These strategies include 1) speakers using their turns at talk to display prior knowledge of the information contained in a previous speaker's utterance (use of the response "I know"), and 2) the use of perceived incompetence in others as a foil for displaying one's own knowledge, for example through the use of challenges.

Finally, this account has isolated certain conversational consequences of these strategies. In particular, it has focused on 1) the occurrence of overlapped utterances generated by residents' displays of knowledge, and 2) repetition of utterances by one speaker or across speakers also generated by knowledge displays.

4.8. Implications

What can be learned from these interactional patterns about the function of conversation for these group home residents? The examples presented here demonstrate that these individuals use their turns at talk to display knowledge, even when this display runs counter to more general conversational rules. In particular, conversation is organized not so much around topic, but rather in terms of speakers' efforts to assert their competence vis-a-vis a particular topic. This is not to say that these speakers are not interested in the pursuit of certain conversational topics in their own right. On the contrary, group home residents routinely initiate conversation around certain areas of enduring interest. However, their *response* to the conversational turns of others is generally in the service of displaying their knowledge of information, rather than furthering the development of a particular topic in conversation.

These interactional patterns stand in contrast to those observed among a similar group of mildly and moderately retarded adults participating in weekly peer counseling/group discussion sessions at a sheltered workshop (Anderson-Levitt, this volume; Graffam, this volume). Unlike the group home, this setting provides participants with a "time-out" from the restrictions and dependent, less-than-adult status that structure their lives outside this context. Emphasis is placed on minimizing incompetence and maintaining social harmony rather than on asserting individual competence in everyday skills. These important differences in the goals inherent in the two settings result in very different patterns of conversational interaction. In the group home, conversation is characterized by discussion of household routines and activities and residents' displays of competence in these areas, generally through announcements and challenges. In the peer counseling/group discussion sessions, on the other hand, conversational interaction centers on the resolution of peer conflict, primarily through the statement of a problem and attribution of blame to particular individuals. (See Anderson-Levitt and Platt [1984] for further discussion of differences between the two settings.)

This conversational evidence of mildly and moderately retarded adults' sensitivity to social context is important for assessing the conversational patterns in interaction between retarded and nonretarded speakers. In many situations in which conversation between two such interlocutors takes place, the competence of the retarded speaker is a primary concern, either explicitly or implicitly (cf. Linder 1978a; Sabsay and Platt, this volume). As in the group home situation, the retarded speaker may use his/her turns at talk to display knowledge/competence in violation of the nonretarded speaker's expectations concerning the organization of conversation, e.g., those related to topic initiation and maintenance.

The notion that conversation may serve different functions not only across settings but across speakers as well has important implications for the way in which the cognitive capacities of mentally retarded individuals are assessed. What appear to be deficiencies in conversational competence may be in fact a strategy for organizing conversation in terms of its function for the retarded speaker in that particular setting. Further observation and recording of spontaneous conversation among retarded speakers is needed to formulate a more complete picture of how cognitive and social constraints influence the patterning of conversational interaction.

5. WEAVING THE CLOAK OF COMPETENCE: A PARADOX IN THE MANAGEMENT OF TROUBLE IN CONVERSATIONS BETWEEN RETARDED AND NONRETARDED INTERLOCUTORS[19]

Sharon Sabsay and Martha Platt

In his study of adaptation to life in the community after release from a state hospital, Edgerton (1967) explored mildly retarded individuals' awareness of the stigma attached to incompetence. He documented these individuals' "often ingenious and always strenuous efforts" (p. 208) to cover themselves with a protective cloak of competence, but observed that "the cloaks that they think protect them are in reality such tattered and transparent garments that they reveal their wearers in all their naked incompetence" (p. 218). These retarded individuals were not alone in their constant attempts to disguise or conceal their incompetence, however; Edgerton found that those with whom retarded individuals interacted, in what he termed a "benevolent conspiracy," strove to avoid embarrassing their retarded interlocutors by not revealing that they were aware of their incompetence, and attempted to help them smooth over or cover up their failings.

In this paper we would like to explore how Edgerton's benevolent conspiracy works in conversation, how interlocutors attempt to help mentally retarded individuals weave their cloak of competence. We will illustrate some of the problems that retarded individuals' intellectual and social deficits create for interlocutors, and the ways in which concern for these persons' self-esteem influences how the resulting communicative and interactional trouble is managed. In the process, we will suggest that this concern with preserving retarded interlocutors' "face" (Goffman 1967; Brown & Levinson 1978) distinguishes these interactions from others in which there is a disparity in the participants' communicative and social competence, such as those between caregivers and young children or between native speakers and foreigners.

For the most part, our observations will be confined to interactions involving nonretarded individuals whose roles in those interactions are defined vis-a-vis their interlocutors' identity as "retarded persons" — researchers, counselors, workshop supervisors, and the like. Insofar as possible, however, we will point out what features of these interactions also obtain in those where the role of the nonretarded participants is not so defined — parents, family friends, strangers, and so forth.

5.1. Some background to the study

To be labeled "mildly mentally retarded" one must have scored between 55 and 69 on a standard test of general intelligence and exhibit some minor deficits in adaptive behavior. These criteria select out of the population a rather heterogeneous group of people. As adults, such individuals may live at home with their parents or siblings, in board and care or smaller family care facilities, or on their own — alone, with roommates, with lovers, or with spouses. Some of them are unemployed, some work in sheltered workshops, and some are competitively employed. Some have a wide network of friends, others are social isolates.

This paper draws on an ethnographic study investigating the community adaptation of mildly retarded young adults. For 18 months, some 100 such persons were visited on an average of once every two or three weeks for periods ranging from one hour to an entire day (see, e.g., Koegel [1982] for a description of this study). The communicative competence of these study participants was one of the four major focuses of this broader study, but for an additional six months, a subsample of forty-eight individuals were visited with equal frequency with an intensive focus on communicative competence.[20] In both parts of the study, individuals were visited in their homes, with their parents and spouses, at their places of employment, in classes; they were accompanied to the bank, the market, the laundramat, the doctor's office, the social security office, shopping malls, and restaurants. Interactions were taperecorded whenever possible and transcripts from these taperecordings have been used to analyze and document various aspects of individuals' discourse (Kernan and Sabsay 1982, 1984; Sabsay and Kernan 1983). Extensive fieldnotes written after each visit provide a wealth of observational detail and contextual information.

5.2. Trouble

Donald began telling me their problems with the landlord and the roaches and

> *the eviction notices. He paced around the room during this explanation and for at least another 15 or 20 minutes. Right away I was having a hard time following his conversation. He'd change topics mid-sentence, he said things that were not at all connected with one another, and he referred to people as "he" or "she" and didn't tell me who he meant. I was rapidly confused and disoriented by his conversation...about what had occurred when, what had caused what to happen, and what stage all the proceedings were in. I also had this problem when I was trying to get information from Donald about his previous residences. He gave me at least three different stories about where he'd lived when....[21]*

Although they do occur, the speech problems so often found in conjunction with more severe degrees of retardation are neither as prevalent nor as troublesome with mildly retarded speakers. Nor are grammatical and lexical deficits a significant problem. More troublesome are the often substantial problems manifested in connected discourse — omission or poor sequencing of information, inadequate referencing, apparently irrelevant or inappropriate conversational contributions, abrupt and unmarked topic changes, and the like — that characterize the talk of many retarded speakers (Kernan and Sabsay 1982, 1984; Sabsay and Kernan 1983). Typical of comments received again and again in fieldnotes, for example, is:

> Kathy didn't tell this story quite as clearly as I just did and it was only through getting several versions of it and my asking her a lot of questions that I finally understood, pretty much anyway, what had happened. Kathy didn't tell the story in order, she kept switching who she meant by "she" and "they," and she often didn't really answer my questions.

Discourse related problems of this type cause listeners problems in understanding. The trouble arising from the conversational behavior of mildly retarded interlocutors, however, goes beyond that of dealing with problems of understanding. Conversational partners must also contend with difficulties of a more purely social nature — with a multitude of rather transparent attempts at impression management, with totally inappropriate behavior, comments, or topics, with incomprehension or feigned comprehension, with displays of mundane knowledge and statements of the obvious, with restricted possibilities for conversational topics, and a variety of other problems, all of which make social interaction awkward, and can give rise to impatience, embarrassment, and distance on the part of nonretarded interlocutors. In this section, we would like to illustrate some of these troublesome conversational behaviors with brief portraits of representative individuals.

Donald. His whiny, high-pitched voice and his constant preoccupation with often self-created problems for which he refuses to take any responsibility whatsoever sometimes make Donald an unpleasant companion. But it is his lack of ability to express himself coherently that gives him away as being retarded, almost from the moment he begins to talk. As the fieldnote excerpt at the beginning of this section documents, Donald's conversation embodies many of the problems found in the discourse of mildly retarded speakers. Rather than attempt to elaborate on the fieldworker's description, we let Donald speak for himself. In the same first visit referred to above, the fieldworker (M) is explaining to Donald (D) the purpose of the research project and why she wants to visit him:

M: ...It's a way of helping other people who have problems who aren't doing as well as you guys are. You guys are doing pretty *well*. Ya have a job 'n' an apartment 'n' all that. And //by]

D: //Yeh]

M: your experience then that helps other people who aren't doing as well ((pause)) That's pretty much what it's about.

D: Well I'm being thrown out, naturally.

M: You *are*?

D: Yeah, I'm trying to save my apartment.

M: How come they're throwing you out?

D: We:lls (couple reasons). (They didn't-) Number one, they didn't fumigate (or anything the building). They go "That's a brand new door there." ((pause)) (And they say-) The guy in one-oh-two smashed the other door.

M: He did? Why?

D: I don't know. Jus' came up here while- Uh we came here one night an' he goes and yells. We didn't do nothin' wrong. We were startin' to go to *sleep*.

M: Huh.

D: (We were   ).

M: Sounds pretty weird.

D: Yeah.

M: So- But why are you- they throwing *you* out then?

D: Because a the *noise*. 'N' an' it's uh first of all it's from ten to uh ten. It's like cooperation up here.* So (then) I go to see a attorney yesterday. About it and that (the hassle) that they be giving me ever since.

M: Huh. They say you're too noisy uh?

* [being cooped up]

The sources of the fieldworker's confusion, evident in her reiteration of her original question and her disfluency as she does so, are clear. Donald switches topics abruptly, does not answer questions relevantly, connects apparently unrelated topics in the same turn, if not in the same sentence, introduces extraneous information, and does not adequately identify referents.

Kathy. Like many of the study participants, Kathy talks repetitively about a very narrow range of personal topics. Kathy's major and minor medical problems, about which she is concerned almost to the point of hypochondria, dominate her conversation. She presents these problems, as she does everything she talks about, almost breathlessly, in run on sentences and incomplete thoughts, introducing them into the conversation with total disregard for their relevance to the ongoing conversation. In the fieldnotes of her visit to Kathy's home, for example, the fieldworker reported:

> [Her father] then offered me another drink and Kathy said, "So I did my deed for the day," ... again referring to the guy in the wheelchair she'd helped on the bus on the way home. This way of jumping back and forth to topics is very typical of Kathy. She did this even more often during dinner. It was more awkward then and more noticeable because the others of us were talking about other things. Right in the middle of something like the weather Kathy would bring up her heart problem again, or she would bring up some little detail about helping the guy on the bus that day. This almost always caused the rest of us to stop talking about whatever we were talking about and created awkward silences. Kathy seemed totally unaware of this awkwardness...She was intent on monopolizing the conversation and telling and retelling all of her stories as fast as she could. She was allowed to tell these stories, but then later, when any of the rest of us made attempts to talk about other things such as what's happening with the youth of today or what's happening in the news, Kathy would break in and bring the conversation back to what's happening to her...Whenever Kathy did this, whatever conversation had been going on just seemed to drop, as if no one knew what to say at that point. I think Kathy's parents were embarrassed by this and embarrassed by the awkwardness it caused.

Marilyn. A picture of Marilyn would show an apparently unexceptional 23-year-old woman. In person, however, her wild gesturing and gangly twisted walk, together with her giggling and her almost preadolescent fascination with movie, rock, and television stars belie this impression. These personalities and fantasied romances constitute almost her entire conversational repertoire. She shows little awareness that others may not share her intense interest and that her favorite topics may not always be appropriate conversational material. The fieldworker, a woman about Marilyn's age, commented:

> I guess what really bothers me about Marilyn's style is her desperately small repertoire of things to talk about. If you're not into big entertainment stars, there is nothing to talk about. Others may feel that all of her detailed knowledge of so many stars in the rock and TV and movie realm is actually quite a vast repertoire. I find it terribly limiting.... Barry Gibb. Maurice Gibb. Robin Gibb. Richard Chamberlin. Rupert Holmes. Miss Piggy. Eddy Rabbit. The Pink Panther. Kermit the Frog. Urban Cowboy. Et cetera, et cetera, et cetera. This is what Marilyn's life literally seems to resolve around. She is a media fanatic who lives largely in a fantasy world. And these obsessions are all that she talks about. At first its cute, then it becomes bearable, and by now it's obnoxious.

Unlike some others in the study, Marilyn does show interest in and attempt to contribute to the topics raised by interlocutors. But her interest is manifested in strings of repeated, trivial questions, that in the end become merely irritating. In obvious exasperation after a long afternoon in Marilyn's company, the fieldworker wrote:

> This was a particularly exemplary visit for pointing out the kinds of petty, silly questions Marilyn frequently asks, about me, husband, my job, my family. I told her we were going to a dance concert tonight. Her question: "You going to dance?" As we drove to the ice cream place, we passed the G_____ Corporation where [my husband] is currently contracting, and I pointed it out to her. Her question:"What are Richard's hours?" "What freeway does he take home?" "Does he like his job?" Later, the dance concert came up again. Her question: "Which car are you going to take, yours or Richard's?" We talked some about the weekend. Her question: "What are your mom and dad doing this weekend?" Then more on the dance concert. "What time is the dance tonight?" I told her about the cake for Nancy and Marsha's birthday that we had at work today. Her question: "What kind of cake?" I told her we were having some friends over for dinner on Sunday night. Her question: "Where do they live?" I mentioned my sister's upcoming birthday. Her question: "Where does she live?" ...I'm convinced a lot of [Marilyn's questions are] just plain filler, a nervous habit of sorts to generate conversation and take the focus off of her.

John. While Marilyn lives a sheltered existence in her parents' home and acts much younger than her age, she does have friends from social groups and special adult classes who share her intense interest in television and music personalities. By contrast, John, at the same age, lives in an apartment with a roommate, has held the same job for several years, does volunteer work at a convalescent home on the weekends, and tries to fill what little leisure time he has with varied activities. He is, however, socially isolated, and his strange mannerisms and interactional style make him appear to be lower functioning that he actually is. Like Marilyn, John's limited repertoire of conversational topics and techniques leads him to ask innumerable questions to hold up his end of the conversation. His question asking, however, has a different quality. He resorts to asking endless streams of questions, some of which are simply bizarre and some of which, it is abundantly clear, he already knows the answers to. For a number of visits, for example, John returned again and again to the topic of boots, questioning the fieldworker persistently about her boots, her mother's boots, her sisters' boots. Of one visit the fieldworder reported:

> John said he was excited about Christmas because we'll have some cool weather then. I asked what else he liked about Christmas and he said "Sometimes it rains, sometimes it shines." He said sometimes he goes to the mountains with his parents at Christmas time. (I think he's heading toward a boot conversation.) John asked if I was going to the mountains this year. I said I didn't know....I asked him if he skied, and he said no. He said he takes his hiking boots. Then he asked if I have hiking boots and if they're like his boots. I said yes I have boots, but I didn't know if they are like his because I haven't seen his. He asked if I wanted to see his boots and I said yes, so he went and got them....He asked me to compare my boots to his. I said I thought mine have a bigger sole. He wanted to know what color my boots are, and I said brown. He asked, pointing to his own shoes, "Are these brown?" I said yes and then asked him if they looked brown to him. He said yes, and then wanted to know if I have any other boots. I said no. He said, "No rain boots?" I said no .... He asked if [my mother] has hiking boots. I said no. He asked if I had any sisters and where they lived....He wanted to know if my sisters had boots. Then he repeated back about my having boots and that they are brown.

In the following excerpt, John pursues the incredibly obvious questions of why one doesn't like to go to the dentist and just what it is that hurts:

> I asked John what he had done that day and he said he worked and had gone to the dentist. I asked if the dentist had found anything wrong with his teeth and he told me his teeth were in perfect condition. That led John to ask "Do you like the dentist?" I told him I didn't, and he said, "You don't? How come?" I told him this was because the dentist hurts me and he said, "Yeah. What hurts? That machine?", and I said, "Yes." Then John wanted to know "What type of machine does he use, that drill?" and I mumbled "yes." That seemed to stop this line of questioning for some reason, or perhaps he had just exhausted the possibilities in the area. It's clear from his questions that

he already knows the answers when he asks them and this seems to be just an exercise in making conversation.

Maureen. Given her daily experiences at work, maintaining a household with her husband, and socializing with friends, one would expect Maureen to have a broad repertoire of conversational topics. While she does speak of her own experiences, her conversation is filled with reports of the experiences, thoughts, and words of others. And, once she overcomes her reticence, her talk is incessant and filled with an inordinate amount of extraneous, trivial detail. This characteristic is a source of frustration and annoyance for her listeners, but, like Marilyn, Maureen appears unaware of the effect that her behavior has on others.

> As I was trying to finally get out the door, Maureen started on some silly story about a cat she used to have, and went on in the same overly detailed inappropriate manner that I have begun to recognize as her pattern.... Everyone knows someone who speaks a mile a minute, who you seem never able to shut up, who has a story for anything you have to say....Maureen's pattern is more difficult to describe, because it also seems characterized by so many empty filler words and such a hyper, nervous energy. Only actual examples would be effective:
>
> M: Yeah, last night Sally called and Sally goes "Is Melody still coming over at ten o'clock?" I go "Yeah, she's still coming over." She has to babysit. Oh, she said that she's been babysitting like a lot, ya know, really a lot, the past few days, like for Christmas and stuff. Even now, she still has to babysit more. Jerry is two years old, and his mom goes "Bye, Jerry, I gotta go now," and he goes, "But what are you going to do? Why can't you stay home?"
>
> D: Wait, who's Jerry?
>
> M: The one that Sally babysits for. He goes, "Why can't you stay home?" Two years old. And she says, "Now, Jerry, I'll tell you what. When you become five years old, I'll stay home more." And he goes, "Good. Goody." Then he goes, "Okay," then he would be happy. Then he would be happier. I mean, he doesn't mind Sally babysitting. It's just that he wants his mommy to stay home too. So this Saturday, she was going to have to babysit, except for one thing. The woman called her last night and told her that they're going to stay home. So she doesn't have to babysit. So she's going to, going to go get a new dress. She wants to get a new dress, and then clean up the house, because her upstairs needs cleaning, and then pick up Gloria at 6 o'clock and then do something with Gloria afterwards.

My reaction to the above anecdote? Who the hell cares! ... there are so, so many unnecessary details that the whole story becomes a joke, a laborious one to listen to at that. The problem is that every single thing that Maureen uttered was in the same vein, where many times it would have been more appropriate for her to respond with a simple "uh huh" or an acknowledgment that she heard you. Rather she would go off on an extensive story of her own on whatever the topic of the moment was. It's not that she strayed from the topic, or even that it's inappropriate to tell of such experiences. It's Maureen's constancy, her rapid pace, and excessive details that makes it become inappropriate.

Carl. Carl's arrogant, belligerent demeanor and know-it-all attitude contrast strikingly with his wife Maureen's timidity and passive, albeit nervous, style.

> Basically, today Carl was very much his usual feisty, authoritative, somewhat bossy, yet humorous self ... there are even times when it seems he has slipped into the same mode with me as he frequently behaves with Maureen — bossy, with an air of superiority, and irritated haughtiness....When we were leaving the bank and he was directing me out of the maze of a parking lot, I made a wrong turn and he yelped, "Not there. I didn't say there." It probably took him great restraint not to finish his tirade with, "you idiot." But it's the exact same attitude he treats Maureen with. And he frequently makes rash generalizations in a chauvinistic vein, such as, after the bank, when I was fishing for my keys at the bottom of my purse, he snapped, "I hate girls with purses. They never know how to organize them." I don't think he realizes how frequently nasty and insulting he comes off as.

But with time, as one gets to know Carl, it becomes apparent that much of this demeanor is bluster, stemming from his constant need to demonstrate his competence and conceal his shortcomings. Ironically, Carl is one of the most competent study participants and quite often it is only his overemphatic and annoying attempts at impression management that call attention to his otherwise unnoticeable deficits. After watching Carl negotiate a transaction at the bank, the fieldworker commented:

> I'm quite sure Carl didn't realize how obnoxious he was sounding. And he got progressively worse, not better. I think Carl's uncomfortable in these situations. He's not great with math and can't read. He overcompensated for his inadequacies by being loud and by trying to be funny. In reality, I think it only drew attention to them. The teller remained mellow and restrained and polite, but I think he realized he was dealing with someone slightly strange.

In these brief portraits we have exemplified some of the conversational behaviors of mildly retarded individuals that cause interactional trouble — inadequate discourse design, inappropriate topic management, limited conversational repertoires, excessive and irrelevant details, and transparent patterns of self-presentation designed to mask incompetence. This is, however, by no means an exhaustive catalog of causes of trouble in interaction.[22]

It should be borne in mind that we are focusing here on troublesome behaviors and the repercussions such behaviors have for conversational interactions, so these portraits emphasize the study participants' least appealing qualities and cast them in a rather unattractive light. In the fieldnote excerpts used here, fieldworkers have vented their exasperation or discomfort in the face of interactional trouble. Other excerpts with a different focus would reveal participants' more attractive qualities, their many areas of competence, and the affection and concern fieldworkers developed for them. Interactions of the types exemplified, however, are clearly troubled. As the quotes from the fieldnotes document, retarded speakers' conversational behavior can give rise to confusion, annoyance, and embarrassment. Interlocutors are faced with the dilemma of somehow dealing with this trouble without endangering the retarded individual's self-esteem and further disrupting the interaction. It is to this problem we now turn.

5.3. Managing trouble

> There are many times in conversation when I get the feeling Marilyn just plain doesn't understand. I'm so used to it I immediately compensate for it by rescuing it with a small explanation or rewording, saving her from ever having to admit that she doesn't understand.

As Edgerton's work demonstrates, for mentally retarded adults the social stigma associated with intellectual incompetence is a basic and inescapable concern. Virtually every social interaction in which they participate is to some degree influenced by this fundamental reality. Therefore, to an extent not characteristic of other interactions between speakers who are not equally competent, actions of others directed at mediating incompetence are potentially face-threatening. Indeed *any* feature of such conversations that suggests that it is other than an interaction between "normals" may prove troublesome. In such interactions, participants may bear the additional burden of de-emphasizing their inequality. As we shall see, this sets up a tension between conversational participants' desire to prevent or minimize trouble and the fact that attempting to do so may in fact give rise to trouble by damaging the retarded person's self-esteem.

Both retarded and nonretarded interlocutors recognize that the conversational interactions they engage in are extremely vulnerable to trouble and they share the common goals of preventing trouble or minimizing it once it does occur. However, retarded speakers are often unaware that listeners are having trouble understanding them, and even of their own lack of understanding of others. Of Donald, for example, the fieldworker commented:

> I'm sure he has no sense that his conversation is not clear, that the way he says things often confuses the listener. I'm sure it never occurs to him that I ask questions because I don't have the foggiest notion of how what he's just said relates to the things he's said previously....

And, like Carl, Maureen, and Marilyn, mentally retarded speakers may be unaware that their behavior is inappropriate.

Although they may be made aware of trouble by some action on the part of interlocutors, retarded individuals may lack the communicative resources and interpersonal skills for dealing with them, as we will illustrate below. And even if retarded speakers are already aware of problems with the interaction, they may be unwilling to acknowledge them, for any acknowledgment of trouble is tantamount to an admission of incompetence. Of one study participant a fieldworker wrote:

> Robin reacts very strongly to being misunderstood. As I've said, she comes on as being very sure of what she says and if you question her, she acts almost offended that you would not understand what she's talking about.

Of another the fieldworker reported:

> Vicky seems to become very impatient when she is not understood, and her speech is not always easy to understand as she has rather childlike speech patterns. She became impatient a couple of times when I didn't immediately understand what she was trying to say. Her way of coping with the matter seems to be to blame the other person for their inability to understand. When this happened I accepted full responsibility for my lack of understanding. It seems we will get along well as long as we continue this arrangement.

Because of retarded speakers' limited conversational skills and their reluctance to acknowledge problems in the interaction, the burden of managing trouble falls primarily on the nonretarded interlocutor and it is their behavior that we will focus on here. (But for discussions of the strategies used by retarded individuals for disguising or compensating for incompetence, see Edgerton [1967] and Linder [1978b].)

As in any conversation, when nonretarded listeners do not understand what retarded speakers say, they ask them to clarify, confirm, or repeat (e.g., Schegloff, Jefferson and Sacks 1977). However, repair is usually difficult and often unsuccessful.[23] Retarded speakers may ignore clarification requests, give further confusing information, or simply fail to grasp their interlocutor's intent. All of these difficulties greatly impede the flow of conversation, as in the following conversation as the fieldworker (K) tries to understand what happened when the participant's boyfriend, Leon, found out that she had plans to go out with someone else, John.

K: All right. It slipped out and Leon told you that, he didn't//want you]

P: //Leon found out]

K: to go out with- All right. Leon found out and he didn't want you to go out with John, so you called up John?

P: Yes, and then I called up- No I called Leon about three o'clock in the afternoon Saturday.

K: All right. But I- You see I sti- What I don't understand is that-((pause)) Did- You didn't cancel the date//with John?]

P: //*No*:::.] I- I-
      We resched- No we didn't reschedule it, we reschedul-rescheduled it the same day it was supposed to be rescheduled.=

K: =All right. Was there a//ny point when-]

P: //Like last Friday]

K: Was the date ever called off?

P: No

P: It was not called off. So why were you calling up John?

P: To apologize.

K: All right. What were you apologizing about.

P: Says, "Sorry what happened John," y'know.

K: About its//slipping] out, an-

P: //About-] About- It's- Not- I didn't apologize because it came out of John's mouth. I didn't have to 'pologize to John. I 'polaged-apologized to John. I told him, "John, I'm really sorry what happened," you know.

K: And what were you referring to.

P: What happened with Leon, y'know. I mean not ( ) why I broke the date. That's what it was.

K: But so you *did* break the date?

P: I di:d. And then we rescheduled it again.

K: Oh, so af- when you called up to-

P: Not for the following week for the same Friday it was 'sposed to be.

K: Right. But so- so you broke the date on- Did you break it on Monday night after the meeting?

P: Yeah. After the meeting.

K: And then you called him up and you apologized for breaking the date?

P: Yeah.

K: And you went on the date anyway?

P: Yeah.

In the face of such difficult and often unsuccessful attempts, and in consideration of their interlocutors' feelings, nonretarded speakers may simply abandon efforts at clarification when there is no great need for understanding a particular piece of information. For example, of a study participant's explanation of what she did in her sheltered workshop, the fieldworker remarked:

> This wasn't at all clear to me and didn't really tell me anything, but I didn't pursue it any further as Hilary sometimes has such a hard time exlaining things that it seems like an insensitive thing to do to keep asking the same things over and over again, especially when it doesn't seem very important.

Sometimes, on the basis of their previous experience with their conversational partners, nonretarded interlocutors may realize that there is no point in attempting clarification in the first place. For example, in reporting an account of an incident described to her by the same study participant who is particularly impaired in her expressive abilities, the fieldworker wrote:

> I told Hilary that I'd heard that she'd been sick. I asked how she was feeling now and what had been wrong with her. She said that she was feeling fine now but earlier she was feeling "dizziness and a um when I don't have- I have a- sometimes I skip my per- my monthly and I get uh and I get hot, I get like that and and and and try to have a (bowel movement) out in upstairs and it's shut. I heard Jack call me he said, 'cause she told me we went to McDonald's she told, she going to come at four o'clock so I want to get before no clock in the bathroom so I couldn't look at the clock." I said "I see," but I didn't really.
> Here's what I think happened....Hilary started to tell me about not feeling good this week because she hadn't gotten her period but what was on her mind was that she had been in the bathroom, with the door shut, having a bowel movement when Jack called for her to come downstairs to see me. She had heard him but wasn't able to leave her task just at the moment and hence Mrs. Anderson had called her again after Jack did, as Hilary didn't respond the first time. Hilary had lost track of the time and even though she knew that I was coming at 4 p.m. as Mrs. Anderson had told her I would, she ended up being indisposed and thus embarrassed when I showed up and she didn't

> come down right away. *I understand this now after listening to the tape and piecing the story together. This certainly wasn't that clear at the time. I was also sure that if I asked for clarification that the story would get even more mixed up.*

The fieldworker's description reflects a strategy commonly adopted by interlocutors in such situations: waiting for the information to come out piecemeal and trying to construct an understanding, like, as one fieldworker put it, "putting together a jigsaw puzzle with some of the pieces missing."[24] In much the same vein, interlocutors often attempt to make the conversation flow as smoothly as possible, despite the incoherence of retarded speakers, by picking up on those threads which do allow some topical coherence — as Donald's fieldworker does with her last comment in the transcript of their conversation above. She disregards all the irrelevant information he introduces and bases her contribution on the most relevant one, the noise: "They say you're too noisy uh?"

Often it is not a concern for the retarded speaker's inability to respond adequately to the repair initiation that prompts nonretarded interlocutors to forego attempts. Instead, it is a concern that the very fact of initiating repair might emphasize or focus attention on incompetence on the part of the retarded speaker. When it is necessary to elicit certain information, however, nonretarded interlocutors simply persevere, all the while realizing that their efforts may ultimately be unsuccessful and may further disrupt the interaction.

As we pointed out in the previous section, managing trouble in interactions goes beyond dealing with problems of understanding to coping with inappropriate or bizarre social behavior. As with problems of understanding, some of the trouble caused by a retarded individual's unusual conversational behavior may be anticipated and to some degree circumvented. For example, of her reaction after a long day with Maureen and her interminable, overly-detailed trivial stories, the fieldworker wrote:

> For a bit of a reprieve, I turned on the car radio and, quite honestly, hoped to keep conversation to a minimum. I was truly tired of Maureen's babbling and developed a strategy by this point of taking care not to initiate much so that no new topics would be introduced for her to babble about....Dummy that I am, I broke the silence, talking about taking naps during the day. Maureen started right up again.

For the most part, however, such problems can only be addressed and smoothed over after the fact.

Nonretarded interlocutors have essentially two options for managing inappropriate or bizarre behavior: they may act as if it were not inappropriate and attempt to rectify the disruption it may have caused in the ongoing interaction, or they may call attention to it and hold the retarded speaker accountable for violating the rules of social conduct. How, for example, do interlocutors deal with John's questions:

> [His mother] calls John on some of his little behaviors and seems to just go along with others. For example, with John's question asking, she usually just keeps answering his questions, just as if it was normal to be asking so many questions and about things he generally already knows the answer to ....Occasionally she would just answer "I don't know," and then try to change the subject, but usually she just answered his questions ....My response to some of John's questions is to say, "What do you think the answer is?" or "I'll bet you know the answer to that one." His mother, however, just continues to answer him with no detectable impatience in her voice.

Parents and service providers (such as counselors, social workers, workshop supervisors, board and care facility operators) often correct the behavior of retarded individuals, holding them accountable for violating rules of appropriate behavior. But corrective actions seem to be more common in situations where nonretarded individuals see themselves in the role of socializing agents. In such situations, individuals see the inappropriate behavior of their retarded interlocutors as a reflection on themselves and therefore as potentially face-threatening for them as well as for their charges. Such corrections may ultimately help retarded speakers present themselves in a more positive light, but they draw attention to the fact that what the retarded speakers are doing is *not* acceptable behavior.[25] In other situations, where nonretarded individuals do not see themselves in this role, inappropriate behavior is seen in a different light. It is viewed as potentially damaging only to the retarded person's self-presentation. At such times, interlocutors enter more fully into Edgerton's conspiracy, helping retarded individuals to present themselves as competent by attempting to smooth over or minimize rather than correct inappropriate behavior. Managing inappropriate behavior in this way was by far the more common approach taken by nonretarded interlocutors in the conversations focused on in this study. We have already seen examples of this approach in the fieldworkers' attempt to smooth over the trouble caused by Donald's incoherence, tolerance of Marilyn's limited conversational interests and trivial questions, and patience in the face of Maureen's incessant babbling.

Thus far we have focused on how nonretarded conversational partners manage on their own behalf the trouble created by their retarded interlocutors' communicative and social behavior. As the quote at the beginning of this section suggests, however, nonretarded conversational participants are sensitive to the fact that retarded individuals have difficulties as listeners as well as as speakers. Consequently nonretarded speakers resort to a variety of strategies to both prevent and repair nonunderstandings on their listeners' part. They may anticipate their listeners' difficulty by simplifying their talk, as caregivers do to young children or native speakers to foreigners, on various levels: syntactic, lexical, topical. Usually nonretarded speakers adjust their talk on the basis of their previous experience with the retarded individual. Fieldworkers, for example, frequently avoided topics they knew their interlocutors were incapable of understanding and contributing to. When nonunderstandings actually occur, nonretarded participants invoke much the same strategies to repair them: they rephrase questions, substitute simpler lexical items, paraphrase statements, abandon nonproductive topics, and so forth.

By adjusting their discourse to their retarded interlocutors' level of understanding, nonretarded speakers help their conversational partners mask their intellectual limitations. They do this in other areas as well, again helping them create performances of competence. Of an incident at lunch with Carl and Maureen and another researcher, Paul, for example, the fieldworker reported:

> In the middle of this, Maureen interestingly interrupted, asking Carl, "Well Carl, did you find your grilled cheese sandwich in there [the menu]?" Carl responded, "Not really. I haven't really looked yet." It seemed unusual for Maureen to put Carl in such a position, as there was actually a tone of intending to embarrass him in the question that she posed. His response was an appropriate one given that he would prefer to cover up the fact that he can't read to people that he doesn't know very well....Paul, I think, knowing of Carl's problem from my notes, casually read the description of the "Swinger-burger" which we were all talking about, as if to help Carl out of the embarrassing spot he was in. Following Paul's cue, I pointed out a few other things and read one or two other descriptions.

So far, we have discussed primarily dyadic interactions. However, there are many instances in our data of multiparty conversations in which a nonretarded participant familiar with the retarded individual intervenes either on the part of the retarded interlocutor or on the part of another, nonretarded participant to smooth over actual or potential trouble. On the basis of a previously acquired understanding of what the retarded interlocutor is trying to say, for instance, a nonretarded speaker might attempt to clarify for a third party, as in the following example:

> George then asked John what kinds of problems he has with his roommate. John answered, "About the bedroom mostly." George inquired, "Well does that mean not keeping it up or what! Making noise or what?" John replied, "Swip swapping it." "What was that?" "Swip swapping." "Oh, I see," said George, not really seeing. John added, "Changing" and I clarified, "Changing bedrooms." George responded, "I see, I see. Why are you doing that?" John answered, "I was pinned up in the big bedroom for a while. So I wanted to change." George responded, "I see." I added, "John used to have the bedroom on the noisier side of the building," and John concurred. George asked, "You didn't like that?" and John answered, "No."

After reporting this conversation, the fieldworker commented: "Though John answered George's questions, he really didn't give him enough information to understand what had gone on. I, of course, jumped in to fill the gap as I was to do for most of the evening."

The previous example illustrates a case of conversational repair intended mainly to facilitate the social interaction, as the content of the conversation was not particularly important and the tone of the occasion primarily social. There are other occasions, however, where understanding is critical and the intervention of a nonretarded speaker can be instrumental. For example, a fieldworker accompanied a study participant, Jeff, to the social security office to observe how he managed to present and resolve the issue of a penalty he had been charged, and reported the following:

> Our first act was to talk to the secretary who takes your name, categorizes your problem, and leads you to your seat....Jeff did not handle this too badly. He identified himself and gave the name of the worker who had helped him last time....He then tried to explain why he was coming in and it was here that he started to drift. His words were all over. He drew on many past incidents that the secretary had no knowledge of which he expected her to understand, and was generally incoherent. So at this point I ...tried to clarify things. Jeff gave me a look of thanks and as we were going to our seats said that he was glad that I spoke because he was starting to lose his cool.

> [Once in the social worker's office] Jeff and I sat down in front of her desk. Jeff showed her his letter and then proceeded to ramble. He brought in this and brought in that and generally had the social worker confused. I mean, she looked at the letter and saw that he was not going to have to pay the remainder of his penalty and was thus unsure why he had come in....Like before, after waiting for a while, until I was sure that Jeff was not being understood, I jumped in. I explained why Jeff thought he shouldn't have to

pay the penalty and why he should be reimbursed and that he wanted to know what the total would be for his future checks.

Nonretarded interlocutors intervene not only to ensure that other nonretarded listeners understand, but also to make sure that retarded participants can follow what is being said. Of the same incident at the social security office the fieldworker wrote:

> While the social worker was out of the room Jeff once again kind of gave me a smile. He seemed to be totally overwhelmed by the process. He said that he didn't understand much of what she was saying because she was "talking too fast and using big words." At this I became aware that I must be a little more active in mediating and also try to have the social worker rephrase things over and over until Jeff understood them.

We have argued that responsibility for managing trouble falls mainly upon nonretarded interlocutors because retarded individuals may fail to recognize that problems have occurred or, if they do, may lack the ability to repair them or feel that acknowledging them might be seen as a damaging admission of incompetence. We have shown that when nonretarded interlocutors do not understand retarded speakers, they may or may not attempt repair, depending on their past experience with the individual and the purpose or content of the conversation. That is, their decision to attempt repair or not and the way they do so is influenced by whether they judge that any attempt will be successful, by the importance of obtaining the information, and by a concern for the fragile self-esteem of their interlocutor. If repair is done at all, it is done subtly and tactfully.

In anticipation of the problems that retarded listeners may have understanding them, nonretarded speakers carefully modify their own talk, gauging the appropriate level of complexity on their perception of their hearer's level of comprehension. As in any interaction, they monitor their listeners for evidence of nonunderstanding as conversation proceeds, and repair their talk as necessary. Nonretarded individuals more familiar with the retarded speakers' particular communicative inadequacies and with the information that is lacking or poorly presented may also manage trouble for them and other nonretarded interlocutors, clarifying the discourse of retarded speakers for others and making sure that their talk in turn is understood by the retarded participants.

Nonretarded individuals also attempt to mitigate for themselves and others the consequences of inappropiate behavior. In the face of such behavior, nonretarded speakers either act as if it were not troublesome, sometimes attempting ameliorative action, or they respond to the behavior with a direct corrective move.

Management of trouble of this type occurs in the context of interactions in which there are participants who are intellectually and socially less competent and therefore less able to manage their own face. Consequently, interlocutors are especially bound to protect them (Goffman 1967: 28). This also hold true, of course, in adult-child interactions. But children have less status than adults and therefore less attention needs to be paid to their face by higher status individuals. In interactions with retarded adults, however, well-intentioned interlocutors seek to maintain the fiction that their conversational partners hold equal status and therefore go to greater lengths to do face-work for them.

5.4. The paradox

The intellectual deficits of mildly retarded individuals are such that, as speakers, they are often unable to adequately structure the content of their conversational contributions for their listeners by discriminating between shared and nonshared, relevant and irrelevant information, by presenting information in coherent sequences, by providing bridges between ideas whose connections are not obvious, and so forth. Consequently, in the interest of maintaining a relatively trouble-free conversation, nonretarded interlocutors must frequently use their turns at talk to reshape the retarded speaker's contribution. The inappropriate behavior of retarded individuals places further stress on the interaction. In smoothing over the disruptions caused by such behavior, nonretarded individuals "repair" the social interaction for themselves and their retarded interlocutors. However, attempts to help retarded speakers weave, if not a cloak of competence, at least a tattered guise of normality, can in fact have the opposite effect.

No matter what one does, there is the potential for negative consequences. Clearly, if one refrains from intervening at all, one leaves the retarded individual exposed in all his "naked incompetence" and guarantees that the interaction will be troubled. The consequences of refraining from any ameliorative or corrective action are apparent in the description of the dinner with Kathy and her parents, where conversation comes to an embarrassing halt. Choosing to intervene, on the other hand, no matter how tactfully, one runs the risk not only of failing to repair the interaction but also of antagonizing or embarrassing the retarded individual by drawing attention to his or her incompetence. In fact, even if one is successful at repairing the trouble and maintaining a smooth interaction, it may be at the cost of making one's retarded interlocutor look more incompetent than he or she is. The more one is unwilling to countenance trouble, the more one may attempt to prevent its occurrence by controlling the direction, content, and level of the interaction. This strategy can be taken to such a point that one does not allow retarded speakers any latitude to display the competence they have and may force them into looking more incompetent than they really are. Take, for instance, the following examples from Linder's (1978b) discussion of a conversation between a workshop supervisor (M) and an adult mildly retarded client about the latter's recent stay at summer camp:

M: And how about dinner?
G: I had some spaghetti.
M: Did you like that?
G: Yes.
M: You like spaghetti?
G: Yes.
M: Great!

M: Oh, okay. Who'd you play [archery] with.
G: With Larry.
M: Larry who?
G: I don't know his last name.
M: He's the one who ate too much?
G: Yes.
M: Is he the kid who ate too much?
G: Yes.
M: Oh!

The purpose of this "incessant repetition and reformulation of both questions and answers", suggests Linder, is chiefly rhetorical. "They are not demands for more information or further interpretation. Rather they are conversational means to remark upon the adequacy of answers, to note and affirm them as appropriate responses" (p.4). Linder concludes:

> Measures such as the above are employed to ensure that one's speech will be relatively unambiguous and are thus intended to both lessen the potential for trouble and to increase the likelihood that one's performance will be a success. Unfortunately, they also assume the incompetence, passivity, and insensitivity of one's respondent ....Ironically, the result is the very thing she

sought to avoid, namely, the unmistakable implication that George is incompetent. The product, i.e., the interview, is relatively smooth and trouble free. Regrettably, the cost is the identification of George as a person unable to cope with the pace, subtlety, and sophistication of normal conversation. [p.6]

Linder's example is hardly an isolated case. Consider Edgerton's (1967) characterization of the reactions of nonretarded speakers to formerly institutionalized mildly retarded individuals.

[T]he normal person who becomes aware of the incompetence of the former patient regularly switches his mode of speech to a condescending tone and a simplified content. The normal person "talks down" and sometimes even attempts a form of "baby talk" as might a colonial Englishman in talking to "native" servants. There is also a tendency for the normal person to speak both more slowly and more loudly than he ordinarily would. Interaction is reduced to a plane upon which the normal person asks few questions, utilizes the simplest possible vocabulary, avoids complexities of humor, and assumes that the former patient has almost no knowledge of what is commonplace, much less what is intricate, in the world. Furthermore, since the normal person generally wishes not to embarrass the retardate, he exercises conspicuous tact. The result is a slowing down of interaction to the point of virtual cessation. [pp. 215-216]

Although our data provide no examples of interactions this extreme, the essence of what Linder and Edgerton describe — a certain well-intentioned condescension — does pervade most interactions between retarded and nonretarded speakers.

5.5. Conclusion

The intellectual and behavioral deficits which in our society lead to the imposition of labels such as "mentally retarded" and "developmentally disabled" are reified by scores on IQ and adaptive behavior tests. As researchers such as Hood, McDermott, and Cole (1980) have observed, however, performances of competence and incompetence are for the most part played out in social interactions, and the behavior of others in such interactions helps create these performances. The accommodations that nonretarded speakers make to less competent interlocutors — such as simplifying and clarifying their own contributions, richly interpreting their interlocutors' contributions, limiting the range of topics raised, or refraining from paying undue attention to inappropriate behavior — may mitigate the consequences of incompetence (Ochs and Schieffelin 1984). By the same token, their responses to the incompetence of their interlocutors may accentuate it (Linder 1978b). Such is the effect, for example, of taking over the telling of a story one thinks a retarded speaker is telling inadequately, controlling interactions through questions on only the most limited and mundane of topics, or remaining silent in the face of inappropriate behavior. On the other hand, responding casually to repetitive and inappropriate questions while continuing to carry on other talk, as John's mother does, subtly modifying one's talk in response to evidence of nonunderstanding, as Marilyn's fieldworker did, and being sensitive to other problems of self-presentation and impression management as Paul and the fieldworker did in Carl's case, help to downplay the retarded speaker's incompetence. Thus, nonretarded interlocutors may help retarded speakers to weave a cloak of competence, and they may also be the ones to unravel it.

FOOTNOTES

1. Almost from the beginning (11/5/75), two separate, regular weekly group meetings have been held, one at 12:00 and one at 2:00 p.m. These have been designated Group #1 and group #2 respectively. Group members attend during the same time slot with the same peers each week, though individual exceptions have been made under special circumstances. For almost two years, Group #2 was divided into two separate sections, each meeting bi-weekly due to overcrowding.

2. The emic or "folk" perspective is a primary research concern. Group members are given license to determine the content and the process of group interaction. Members establish priorities and protocol and are considered informed participants or resident-experts. A fact that makes the study of these group meetings so interesting is that these meetings are, in large part, what the client-members have conceived and made them to be. Hence, the meetings more or less accurately reflect client concerns, interaction styles, etc.

3. Aside from the expression of norms and values relevant to the society at large, there are a number of generally informal, yet widely held and expressed rules of social comportment which are relevant to life within the workshop client peer-culture. This is not meant to imply that such social rules are exclusive to the workshop setting or that they diverge significantly from societal rules of etiquette, only that the identified informal social rules have special relevance within this population and setting.

4. A lack of social stimulation and an expressed concern with boredom have been identified as common characteristics of the social lives of workshop clients (Graffam and Turner 1984). Eventfulness is a highly valued quality of life, and eventfulness-raising displays are thought to not only alleviate boredom, but also to contribute in some cases to the presentation of one's social identity and to the maintenance of self-esteem.

5. Personal problems are not simply and always negatively valued by workshop clients. Quite frequently, problems are reported almost exuberantly. In general, such "problems" are fabricated or exaggerated, but occasionally very real, even quite profound problems are accorded such positive responses. Personal problems with presumably negative valence can be somewhat rewarding to a client in that they provide attention and support from others, both of which are positively valued. Furthermore, personal problems are recognized as part of the lives of normal adults, and having problems can legitimize one's status as a grown-up.

6. The study depends heavily on insights about Workshop Society shared by Jim Turner and his colleague Joe Graffam. I also owe thanks for comments and suggestions to Sharon Sabsay; to Ronald Gallimore, Keith Kernan, and members of their seminar on "Interactional Bases of Speech and Cognition" (Fall 1982); and to Michael Moerman and members of his seminar on "Social Interaction" (Winter 1983). Dr. Sabsay and members of Dr. Moerman's seminar helped me with the transcription. Emanuel Schegloff gave early advice on taping and analyzing. Finally, thanks to Frank Marlowe for operating the videocameras and making copies of the tapes.

7. The transcript which follows is excerpted from the transcript in the Appendix. Numbers on the

left margin are line numbers. As noted in the Appendix, "Jo," "Ph," and "Ti" are abbreviations for John, Phil, and Timmy. Brackets joining two lines indicate that the bracketed material was uttered simultaneously. Empty parentheses represent utterances which could not be transcribed.

8. Unfortunately, one client of particular interest here, John, entered the meeting a few minutes late, sitting at the far end of the room, and the stationary camera was not repositioned to include him in its scope. However, his speech was audiorecorded, and Marlowe's mobile camera focused on him when he made his important "speeches."

9. According to transcript conventions, words in parentheses indicate uncertainty on the part of the transcribers. In this quote, Phil was referring to the fact that some researchers make notes in red hardbound diaries.

10. Goffman, alluding to moves in Wittgenstein's "language games," defines a "move" as "any full stretch of talk or its substitute which has a distinctive unitary bearing on some set or other of the circumstances in which participants find themselves" (1976: 24). Cf. Labov and Fanshel's (1977) broad concept of "speech acts."

11. Tharp, Gallimore, and Calkins (1984) identify six strategies for "other-regulation" in Vygosky's sense: instruction (i.e., giving directives), cognitive structuring, regulatory questioning, modeling, contingency management (i.e., rewards and punishments), and feedback. The strategy discussed here is a good example of "modeling." Phil's earlier strategy of demolishing John's premises began with "regulatory questioning," and his restructuring of John's perception of Randy is an example of "cognitive structuring."

12. During the weeks in which I collected data, a particular question of "fact" often identified those clients who sided with Randy and those who sided against him. The "fact" to be debated was whether Randy and Sandra Castle were cousins. The background seemed to be that Sandra Castle, who was married to someone else, was perceived to be behaving like Rodney's girlfriend. Those who would defend Sandra and Randy against any claim of immorality argued that Sandra and Randy were cousins; this explained why they spent time together and seemed to be affectionate. Rather than debating on the basis of known or determinable facts, however, a client tended to argue that Randy and Sandra either were, or were not, cousins depending on whether the client wished to take a stand for or against Randy. Thus reasoning and argumentation were put into the service of social interaction. Interestingly, clients were not consistent in condemning Sandra's apparent extramarital affairs. In the June 2 meeting, they defended her friendship with a different man, illustrating all the more strongly how much the Sandra-and-Randy-as-cousins issue simply served the social maneuverings which were going on.

13. One might argue that John's position weakens even earlier. In his first response to Phil (line G:13), John describes himself in the active voice: "We been to skrool [school] with him." In his second response, though (lines G:28-29), John casts himself as the passive recipient of someone else's action: "Because, because his girlfriend told me--." Distancing oneself from the source of the action can represent a degree of backing off from a strongly held position (Michael Moerman, personal communication).

14. The careful reader may object that just prior to this negative comment about Randy, John had again raised the issue of rumors (lines G:86-88: "An' why is Penny Cole, um:, making rumors about (Randy's parents)?"). This might be interpreted as a continuing defense of Randy against his detractors. If so, it would mean that John still placed himself within Randy's camp at that point. However, I would claim that John's alliance is not the issue here; rather he is obliquely referring to a problem which he already obliquely discussed in the previous episode, Episode F. The real issue, as I will argue later, is that Timmy in under suspicion of spreading "rumors" about Randy.

John makes the remark in line G:86-88 in a further attempt to resolve that issue.

15. On the other hand, Phil might have been treating John as the spokesman for Timmy, and Timmy's reluctance to talk might be explained by his speech defect, or by the fact that he kept his back turned during most of Episode G. However, while the evidence cited here is ambiguous, I believe the evidence cited below from Episode F confirms that John and Timmy did perceive a rift between Timmy and Randy.

16. We will be able to address this question after comparing our findings about this workshop with other on-going ethnographic studies of sheltered workshops, including the current study by Padin-Rivera et al. (1983).

17. I.Q.'s of two residents are recorded as "moderate" and "high end of mild."

18. Parentheses surrounding a word or phrase indicate a tentative transcription; empty parentheses, '(   )', indicate the utterance was unclear. False starts and interruptions are indicated by a single dash, '—'. When one speaker's utterance is followed abruptly by another speaker's, without the normal slight pause, a '=' is shown at this point. Pauses are shown in several ways. A comma, ',', indicates a slight pause at grammatical boundaries, e.g., between clauses; a series of two or three periods, '..' or '...', is used to indicate pauses which are longer and/or which do not occur at grammatical boundaries; a pause of greater length, several seconds, is indicated by the word 'pause' enclosed in double parentheses. Double parentheses are also used to indicate nonverbal or prosodic information, e.g., ((loud)) or ((slaps table)). Overlapping utterances are marked at the beginning of the overlap with double slash marks, '//', and at the end with a bracket, ']'. A bracket on the lefthand margin of the transcript, '[', is an additional indication of where overlap occurs. Turns at talk are labeled with numbers in the lefthand margin.

19. We wish to thank fieldworkers Marsha Bollinger, Melody Davidson, Pauline Hayashigawa, and David Tillipman for their insightful observations and sensitive portrayals of study participants. We also wish to acknowledge our incalculable debt to the many annonymous individuals who allowed us to observe and participate in their lives.

20. The four components of the Community Adaptation of Mildly Retarded Persons study were: Lives in Process; Communicative Competence; Everyday Thought and Reasoning; and Socio-Emotional Adjustment.

21. Fieldnote excerpts have been lightly edited in some cases for grammar, spelling, and continuity.

22. We don't mean to claim that the behaviors described are unique to or diagnostic of mentally retarded individuals. Instead, it is the occurrence of a constellation of these behaviors, and the frequency with which they occur, that sets these persons apart from their nonretarded counterparts. We have singled out these particular behaviors, which might be potentially troublesome in any interaction, for purposes of illustration.

23. The obvious comparison here is to the work caregivers do in interpreting the utterances of young children, but what adult mildly retarded speakers are attempting to convey is usually far more complex than anything children attempt. With young children, adults are usually faced with interpreting the intent of one- or two-word utterances, not with understanding complex circumstances, for example, being evicted from one's apartment.

24. Details may emerge after several retellings of the same account; sometimes, as Graffam (this volume) documents, they may come out over a period of weeks.

25. In certain settings, the emphasis on the acquisition and demonstration of appropriate know-

ledge and behavior is so great that the conversational behavior of retarded individuals is dominated by overt displays of competence. See Platt (this volume) for discussion.

REFERENCES

Anderson-Levitt, Kathryn and Martha Platt
    1984   "The speech of mentally retarded adults in contrasting settings." *Socio-Behavioral Group Working Papers* No. 28, Mental Retardation Research Center, University of California, Los Angeles.

Bedrosian, Jan and Carol Prutting
    1978   "Communicative performance of mentally retarded adults in four conversational settings." *Journal of Speech and Hearing Research* 21:1.79-95.

Brown, Penny and Steve Levinson
    1978   Universals in language usage: Politeness phenomena. In Esther N. Goody (ed.), *Questions and politeness*. Cambridge: Cambridge University Press, 56-289.

Cole, Michael
    1983   "The zone of proximal development: When culture and cognition create each other." *CHIP Technical Report* No. 106. La Jolla: University of California, San Diego.

Cole, Michael, Lois Hood and Ray McDermott
    1982   "Ecological niche picking." In U. Neisser (ed.), *Memory observed*. San Francisco: W.H. Freeman, 366-373.

Edelsky, Carol
    1981   "Who's got the floor?" *Language in Society* 10:3.383-421.

Edgerton, Robert B.
    1967   *The cloak of competence: Stigma in the lives of the mentally retarded*. Berkeley: University of California Press.

Edgerton, Robert B. and Sylvia M. Bercovici
    1976   "The cloak of competence: Years later." *American Journal of Mental Deficiency* 80:5.485-497.

Goffman, Erving
    1967   *Interaction ritual: Essays on face-to-face behavior*. Garden City: Anchor Books.

    1981   "Replies and responses." In *Forms of talk*. Philadelphia: University of Pennsylvania Press, 5-77.

Goodenough, Ward H.
    1971   "Language, culture and society." *Addison-Wesley modular publication* No. 7.

Graffam, Joseph and Jimmy L. Turner
    1984   "Escape from boredom: The meaning of eventfulness in the lives of clients at a shel-

tered workshop for mentally retarded adults." In Robert B. Edgerton (ed.), *Lives in process: Mildly retarded adults in a large city*. (=Monographs of the American Association on Mental Deficiency, No. 6.) Washington, D.C.: AAMD, 121-144.

Grice, H.P.
    1975   "Logic and conversation." In Peter Cole and Jerry L. Morgan (eds.), *Syntax and semantics, Vol. 3: Speech acts*. New York: Academic Press, 41-58.

Heber, R.
    1961   "Modifications in the manual on terminology and classification in mental retardation." *American Journal of Mental Deficiency* 66:4.499-500.

Hood, Lois, Ray McDermott and Michael Cole
    1980   "'Let's *try* to make it a good day' — some not so simple ways." *Discourse Processes* 3:2.155-168.

Hymes, Dell
    1972   "Models of the interaction of language and social life." In John J. Gumperz and Dell Hymes (eds.), *Directions in sociolinguistics: The ethnography of communication*. New York: Holt, Rinehart and Winston, 35-71.

Kernan, Keith T. and Sharon Sabsay
    1982   Semantic deficiencies in the narratives of mildly retarded speakers. *Semiotica* 42:2.169-193.

    1984   "Getting there: Directions given by mildly retarded and nonretarded adults." In Robert B. Edgerton (ed.), *Lives in process: Mildly retarded adults in a large city*. (=Monographs of the American Association on Mental Deficiency, No. 6.) Washington, D.C.: AAMD, 27-42.

Koegel, Paul
    1982   *Rethinking support systems: A qualitative investigation into the nature of social support*. Doctoral dissertation, University of California, Los Angeles.

Labov, William and David Fanshel
    1977   *Therapeutic discourse*. New York: Academic Press.

Langness, Lewis L.
    1976   *Sociocultural aspects of mental retardation*. Unpublished paper, Socio-Behavioral Research Group, Mental Retardation Research Center, University of California.

Linder, Steve
    1978a   "Language context and the evaluation of the verbal competence of the mentally retarded." *Socio-Behavioral Group Working Papers* No.1, Mental Retardation Research Center, University of California, Los Angeles.

    1978b   "The perception and management of 'trouble' in normal- retardate conversations." *Socio-Behavioral Group Working Papers* No. 5, Mental Retardation Research Center, University of California, Los Angeles.

Mercer, Jane
    1973   *Labeling the mentally retarded: Clinical and social system perspectives on mental retar-*

dation. Berkeley: University of California Press.

Meyers, C. Edward, Kasuo Nihira and Andrea Zetlin
1979   "The measurement of adaptive behavior." In Norman Ellis (ed.), *Handbook of mental deficiency, psychological theory and research* (2nd edition). Hillsdale, N.J.: Lawrence Erlbaum Associates, 431-482.

Ochs, Elinor
1979   "Transcription as theory." In Elinor Ochs and Bambi Schieffelin (eds.), *Developmental pragmatics*. New York: Academic Press, 43-72.

Ochs, Elinor, and Bambi Schieffelin
1984   "Language acquisition and socialization: Three developmental stories and their implications." In R. Shweder and R. LeVine (eds.), *Culture theory: Essays on mind, self, and emotion*, Cambridge: Cambridge University Press, 276-320.

Owings, Nathaniel A. and M.D. McManus
1980   "An analysis of communication functions in the speech of a deinstitutionalized adult mentally retarded client." *Mental Retardation* 18:6.309-314.

Padin-Rivera, Edgardo, Helen Maurer, John R. Newbrough, Jacques Page and Celeste G. Simpkins
1983   *That's the way they do: The clique, the leaders, and a work group of mentally retarded adults*. Paper presented at the 16th annual Gatlinburg conference on Research in Mental Retardation and Developmental Disabilities, Gatlinburg, TN, March.

Price-Williams, Douglass and Sharon Sabsay
1979   "Communicative competence among severely retarded persons." *Semiotica* 26:1.35-63.

Sabsay, Sharon and Keith T. Kernan
1983   "Communicative design in the speech of mildly retarded adults." In Keith T. Kernan, Michael J. Begab and Robert B. Edgerton (eds.), *Environments and behavior: The adaptation of mildly retarded persons*. Baltimore, MD: University Park Press, 263-294.

Sacks, Harvey, Emanuel A. Schegloff and Gail Jefferson
1974   "A simplest systematics for the organization of turn-taking for conversation." *Language* 50:4.696-735.

Schegloff, Emanuel, Gail Jefferson and Harvey Sacks
1977   "The preference for self-correction in the organization of repair in conversation." *Language* 53.361-327.

Schegloff, Emanuel A. and Harvey Sacks
1973   "Opening up closings." *Semiotica* 7:4.289-327.

Schiefelbusch, Richard L. (ed.)
1972   *Language of the mentally retarded*. Baltimore: University Park Press.

Schieffelin, Bambi
1979   "Getting it together: An ethnographic approach to the study of the development of

communicative competence." In Elinor Ochs and Bambi Schieffelin (eds.), *Developmental pragmatics*. New York: Academic Press, 73-108.

Tharp, Roland, Ronald Gallimore and Roderick Calkins
  1984   "Relacion entre el autocontrol y el control por otros." *Avances en Psicologia Clinica Latinoamericana* 3:1.45-58.

Turner, Jimmy L.
  1983   "Workshop society: Ethnographic observations in a work setting." In Keith T. Kernan, Michael J. Begab and Robert B. Edgerton (eds.), *Environments and behavior: The adaptation of mildly retarded persons*. Baltimore, MD: University of Park Press, 147-171.

Turner, Jimmy L., Keith T. Kernan and Susan Gelphman
  1984   "Speech etiquette in a sheltered workshop." In Robert B. Edgerton (ed.), *Lives in process: Mildly retarded adults in a large city*. (=Monographs of the American Association on Mental Deficiency, No. 6.) Washington, D.C.: AAMD, 43-71.

Wertsch, James V.
  1979   "From social interaction to higher psychological processes: A clarification and application of Vygotsky's theory." *Human Development* 22:1.1-22.

  1981   "Trends in Soviet cognitive psychology." *Storia e Critica della Psicologica* 2.219-295.

APPENDIX A

Stan:	Where's the rest of the nation? ((repeated 3 times)) We rode our bikes to work today. I gotta steer Ken's [his brother] home. He left it here.
Brad:	I gotta go to work. Gil needs me to stack boxes.
Deac:	Tell him [Jim Turner] your problems then get out.
Stan:	Don Snitch broke those containers. Yesterday. ((group laughter))
Deac:	I heard about it. ((repeated 3 times)) I don't need a broken record. Don Snitch broke some containers yesterday.
Stan:	He got suspended.
Edie:	His wife was crying too.
Deac:	Sure she was!
Edie:	I feel sorry for her.
Stan:	Did he break up his marriage?
Deac:	No! Not yet! ((many voices echo Deac's denial with gusto))
Stan:	He's going to!
Deac:	No he isn't. ((the rest agree heartily)) He's not going to!
Rick:	No. He gonna take this ring forever.
Deac:	That's true. ((several agree heartily)) He's mean and nasty, he swears.
Several:	I know!
Deac:	She's not here because Don's not here.
Rick:	Well what happened? She get suspended?
Deac:	No, Don did so she stayed home.
Rick:	Don got suspended, ha! That's his fault. You never swear in the workshop.
Deac:	Yes, he does. He says goddamnit and all that stuff. He does.
Edie:	Hey! Watch your mind kid!
Stan:	Hallelujah!
Deac:	No, he don't say hallelujah. ((much laughter))
((Two members of the group, routinely tardy due to special work schedules, enter))	
Roger:	Hey! Now we're early and he's late today!
Deac:	He came in, plugged it [taperecorder] in and left.
Stan:	Hold it! Where's the nation? Where's the rest of our nation? The whole nation must be here.
Deac:	Jim walked out the door before Roger and Rudy got here.
Roger:	Lock the door! ((someone does this and much laughter follows))
Deac:	No, don't do that! Lonnie, unlock that door! Don't lock the door.
Stan:	Where's the rest of the nation? The whole nation must be here!
((Jim Turner now enters the room.))	
Deac:	There's Jim. You're late.
Stan:	The whole nation must be here!
Penny:	Jim? I had my birthday party. Got new earrings.
Deac:	You should give some to me.

Rick: Men wear them too.

Deac: I know.

Stan: Men wear them all the time. My dad wears one.

Deac: He should get his ears pierced.

[Brad's supervisor enters, seeking him. Brad apologizes and goes to work, briefly explaining his new job to Jim Turner. Action then continues.]

Penny: You know what my brother did? In the wine, punch!

Jim T: Did you get drunk?

Penny: Some. Fun.

Rick: My mom is going to the airport Sunday to see my Grandpa. I go with her at 10 o'clock. I'm going with my dad.

Jim T: Where's your dad going?

Rick: To the airport to take my mom.

Jim T: You and your dad are staying here?

Rick: Mom is going to the airport to see Grandpa. It's important to me. He's been sick a long time. He went to the hospital one time with sunfever. You know, people get sunstroke. People die from it real easy. He passed out. He's blind, he lost his memory, everything. He's all alone. His wife's gone, died. He's had a hard life. You miss somebody and you love somebody. You know what I mean?

Jim T: Is he in the hospital?

Rick: No, a convalescent home in San Francisco. It's serious important to me. I miss him if he's gone.

Edie: I went to San Diego on vacation. And we had a family reunion. I had fun dancing and everything. Then I danced with my friend and got real tired.

Jim T: How'd you get the black eye?

Edie: My cousin. He's strong, he goes to school. I was playing with him, he got mad at me and hit me. Bam! It still hurts. I got black and blue. I cried, it hurt, and his mother told him, "Stop it!" I had a headache too from it.

Penny: You know where I go Sunday morning? Go to the zoo in San Diego. I see you [Yvette] on Sunday. The tiger come out.

Jim T: Was she there? What were you doing there Yvette?

Deac: Speak up! ((much laughter by the group))

Edie: Did you have fun?

Penny: Tiger. Tiger come out.

Yvette: He's [her boyfriend] got a new bus now.

Jim T: He got a new bus?

Yvette: Ya, a brand new bus, a blue one.

Jim T: Is it one of those very large buses or

Yvette: A small bus, it's his own bus.

Deac: It holds 9.

Jim T: So he can take people around in it.

Penny: Him fun. Him funny on the bus.

Jim T: What's funny about him? Does he tell jokes or

Yvette ((Penny echoes)):   Mmmm hmm. ((indicating "Yes"))

Jim T: He makes everybody laugh huh? What kind of jokes does he tell? Not dirty jokes I hope. ((tongue in cheek))

Yvette: Ya, some dirty jokes.

Stan: You like dirty jokes? Dirty jokes about ostriches coming out of communist China?

Jim T: Ostriches coming out of communist China? Is there a joke about that?
Stan: No, that's no joke!
           [meeting continues for approximately 45 minutes]

APPENDIX B

Transcripts of Episodes F, G, and L

Transcription Conventions

In general, this paper uses a simplified version of the conventions presented in Sacks, Schegloff, and Jefferson (1974), although this conversation was not transcribed in nearly enough detail to bear rigorous conversational analysis.

Words in parentheses, e.g., "(dead)," indicate that the transcribers were not certain or did not agree about the words contained therein. Empty parentheses, e.g., "(   )," indicate that the transcribers could not reconstruct at all something which was said; the length of the empty space gives some subjective sense of the length of the untranscribed utterance. Empty parentheses located where the code for a speaker's name should be, i.e., "( ):," indicate that transcribers could not identify who made the utterance.

Numbers in parentheses, e.g., "(1.0)," indicate a pause timed in seconds. Brief, untimed pauses may be indicated by a period enclosed in parentheses, i.e., "(.)."

Double parentheses indicate gestures, e.g., "((nods))," or qualities of the verbal material which were not transcribed, e.g., "((speeding up))."

Underscoring indicates loudness or high pitch for emphasis. A degree sign (°) marks a softly spoken utterance. A colon, e.g., "uh:", indicates a stretched out sound.

When two or more speakers spoke at the same time, I have employed the ordinary convention of linking the overlapping utterances with brackets. (For example, see the first three lines of Episode F.) However, this convention was not adequate for a situation with over a dozen possible speakers. Therefore, I also adapted a transcription style from Edelsky (1981). Edelsky places the words of the speaker who has the floor in the center of the transcript, and lines up simultaneous comments by other speakers on left- and right-hand columns. I had space for only one side column, and in any case did not want to unravel exactly who had the floor in many ambiguous cases. Therefore, in this transcript, the main conversation occupies the left two-thirds of the page, and side conversations, that is, remarks (or non-verbal communication) which is clearly peripheral to the main topic being discussed, occupies a narrow column on the right. As in Edelsky, *utterances printed on the same line of type indicate simultaneous, i.e., overlapping, speech.* For example, on line 55 of Episode F, Norman is saying, "Who--who's--," at the same time as Timmy is saying, "Who did it?"

Key to Speakers
Ph= Phil
Jo= John
Ti= Timmy
Lu= Lucille
Na= Nancy
Jn= Joan
No= Norman

Al= Alan
Ma= Marie
Mi= Mitchell
JT= Jim Turner (researcher)
JG= Joe Graffam (researcher)
KA= Katie Anderson-Levitt (researcher)

Episode F   *Side conversations*

```
 1 Ph:  (Both) (    ) (can't stand) (    ).
        [                              ]
 2 Ti:  ((looking at John . . . . . . . . . . .))
                         [          ]
 3 Jo:                   Uh, Timmy?
 4 Ti:  I wanna know.
 5 Jo:  Let me say--lemme say it, O.K.?
 6      Suzette--give me the microphone
 7      please.
 8 Na & Jn: ((pass mike to John.))                No:  I wanna talk,
        [                      ]                        [ I wanna talk,
 9 Ti:  (                      )                   Na:  [ ((clap,
                                                          clap))
10                                                 No:  all right,
11 Ti:  I wanna know.                              Ma:  (Jus' wait.)
12                                                 (  ): Shhhh!
13                                                 Al:  Norman!
14 Jo:  That's why I wrote it down                 No:  ((gestures))
                                                   Jn:  [((twd Alan))
15      there,                                     (  ): [Sh!
16      you guys.
17      O.K.
18      Number one
19      (1.0)
20      is:
21      I'll start with Timmy's speech.
22      O.K., Tim?
23 Ti:  ((nods))
24 Jo:  ((reading)) This is a-about some-
25      one who's spreading rumors about          Ph:  ((smiles and waves to ?))
26      Randy Roe. It says here, a--
27      It says here:
28      Would you don't say anything to
29      hurt Leslie and Randy Roe?
30      And (two/to) same thing to his
31      parents. They are all really
32      (dead). Don't wake them up. They
33      are sleeping. They need rest, and
34      don't bother (him). Don't tease
35      Randy about his parents. It's
```

36   his family. He miss them.
37   ((whispering)) O.K.
38   ((reading)) Number two: I know
39   you. I don't lie to my friends.
40   To be your friend that I know how
41   we feel about our friends
42   (from John Dell).
43   ((spoken)) O.K.
44   He-here's something about Penny Cole
45   ((reading)) Is (now) our friend.
46   And why is Penny Cole not your
47   friend? Cause Penny Cole was not
48   our problems.
49   That I have·made my own mind that
50   Jenny ((speeding up, naturally))
51   is really good to me--I like it.
52   (3.0) ((hugs Jenny))
        [   ]
53 Na: ((chuckles, claps))
54 Jo: An--
        [   ]
55 Ti: Who did it?   No: Who--who's--
56 Jo: An' I don't know *why* that   (   ).
57   ((reading)) Penny Cole telling Timmy
58   (what) — what — (pause)
59   I don't know why Penny Cole said that
60   to you about Randy's parents.   No: °Microphone.
61   Why?   ((gestures to
        [   ]
62 Ti: (Penny--)   mike))
63   Jn: ((takes mike from John))
64   No: ((holds hand out for mike))
65 Ti: (Penny Cole said it to me?)
66 Jo: Penny Cole
67   Is she--   Al: ((raises hand for mike))
        [   ]
68 Ti: I *told* you.
69 Jn: ((gives mike to Timmy))
70 Jo: Is Penny Cole saying to you that
71   Randy's parents are dead?
        [   ]
72 Ti: ((gets mike, holds it low))   Al: ((lowers hand))
73 Ti: Pe'y Cole said (to) Randy Roe.
74 Jo: Penny Cole said it, right?
75 Ti: Yes.
76   Not (me).
        [   ]
77 Jo: O.K.
78   (1.0)

79   An' Penny Cole wants you to say it.
80   That's right. I know.
81   *But*, why is he doin' to that for,
82   (huh)?
83 Ti: Who?
84 Jo: Penny Cole.
85 Ti: Because Randy Roe is (   )
86   (something about me, thinking) about
87   me.
88   (2.0, during which John sighs?)
89 Ti: I'm not lying, John.
        [   ]
90 No: That's ridiculous.

Episode G (follows immediately after line F-90)
 1 Jo: It says here--
        [   ]
 2 Ph: I got a question for
 3   you two. My question I wanna say
 4   is--
 5 Jo: Yes?
 6 Ti: ((sigh))
        [   ]
 7 Ph: Uh--
 8   ((calmly)) Is he's your friend,
 9   Randy Roe?
10 Ti: Yes.
11 Jo: Yes.
        [   ]
12 Ph: Why?
13 Jo: Why? Because we been to skrool
        with him.
14 Ph: "*Screwed*"?
15 Jo: School.
16 Al?: School.
17 Lu: Goin' to school together.
18 Ph: ((more derisively)) *I* don't care
        who he go to school with you.
19 Jo: Oh. Kay.
20 Ph: I'm--I feel like (he actin' very
21   stubborn baby). Why you wanna
22   go with him (all the time)?

                                                Mi: [((walks out))
                                                No: ((takes mike))

23   (   ) (he'll get) you two   No: ((into mike)) I wanna talk
                                                     (to you), Philly.
24   (   ) trouble.   Al: ((takes Mi's place))
                                                     May I join you, fellas?
25 Jo: (   )

	No: ((shakes finger & smiles at Joan))
26 Ph: Why you runnin' around with him	
27 all the time?	( )
28 Jo: Because, because his girlfriend	
29 told me-	
30 Ph: ((more vehemently)) *I* don't care	Al?: ( ) ( ): (Yeah, I'm all right.)
31 Leslie think. Leslie is not a boss.	
32 Jo: Leslie told me that she wants me to	
33 go with Randy Roe, not Timmy.	
34 Ph: Don't listen t'her--(to her).	
35 ((speechifying)) *You* got a mind for	
36 your own, *Timmy* got a mind for his	
37 own. (pause)	
38 And why you two wanna make friends	
39 with him? ((keeping gaze on John))	
40 (4.0)	
[ ]	
41 Jn: ((murmurs))	
[ ]	
42 Ti: ((turns his back pointedly and keeps it turned until Episode I))	
43 Ph: I *like* you two.	No: ((raises, lowers hand))
44 Jo: Thank you.	
45 Ph: I really do. I don't want Randy Roe	
46 gets you in trouble.	
47 *I* don' like (the way) he's acting.	No: ((raises, lowers finger))
48 To me he acts so big he not--he	
49 not--he's not (alive).	No: ((blows into mike))
50 He say, ((mocking imitation))	
51 "*I* got *mus*cles" ((imitating	
52 Randy showing his biceps)).	
53 He hasn't.	
54 He think (he Mr. Big in)	No: ( )
55 that line.	( ): Sh!
56 I don't care what Leslie Samson got	
57 a boyfriend that's like *that*.	
58 (4.5)	
[ ]	
59 Jo?: ((murmur))	
60	No: Jim? Ahem.
61 Ph: I--I like Timmy. Timmy's a nice	
62 person.	No: Ahem.
63 An' you, too.	
64 Jo: Thank you.	No: Hello. Hello.
65 Ph: An' Connie's a nice (.)	
66 ((grinning, speeding up))	
67 sexy gal.	
68 Na, others: ((laugh))	

69   No: Jim!
70 Jo: Well, I know she is.
71 Ph: An' Marie is, too.
72 Na: ((murmur))
73 Ph: Sexy and
74   (   ). ((pinching Marie))
        [   ]
75 Lu: Are you tryin' to ignore
76   me, pretenting that I'm not even
77   there?
78 Ka, others: ((laugh))
                 [   ]
79 Ph: No, you are,
80   you are there. ((smiling broadly))

                                            No: ((whispers to Lu)) No,
81 Na: ((laughs))   you're not there.
82 Ph: An: the main reason-- ((pointing to
        Lucille, addressing John))
83   *she* had a problem with Penny Cole
84   *and* Randy Roe!   Al: ((to Joe)) Jim?
85   No: Can I talk, Jim?
86 Jo: An' why is Penny Cole, um:,   Al: Joe? ((points
                                                   to self, mike))
87   making rumors about   To me, O.K.?
88   (Randy's parents)?   JG: ((nods))
        [   ]
89 Ph: Don' listen to
90   Penny. Penny (Cole is a brat).
91 No: Thank you, Phil.
92 Ph: An' she like to make people in
93   trouble, including Marie. ((To
94   Marie:)) An' I want you to keep
95   away from her! I mean it!
96 Ma: ((sigh?))
97 Ph: If she wants to does very bad
98   things, *she* gonna be in trouble.
99   Not you.
        [   ]
100 Jo: I--
101 Ph: An' nobody else.
102 No: Thank you.
        [   ]
103 Jo: I have
104   something else to say to you,
105 Ph: All right.
106 Jo: Mister--
107 Ph: Alman.
108 Jo: Allen.
        [   ]

109 Na: ((laugh))
         [   ]
110 ( ): His name is Alman.
111 No: Mr. Alman. Go ahead.
112 Jo: Randy Roe sometime act, uh
113   (pause)
114 Ph: ((smiling, pleased with self)) A
115   little kid.
116 Jo: No, not a kid. *Mean*, still, like
117   he's--very--*meany*--to my brother;
118   Dennis Valerio's
119   my brother.
         [   ]
120 Ph: (This--)
121   (This time Randy Roe, said to him,)
122   "Buzz off. Leave my   No: ((blows into mike))
123   brother alone."   No: ((into mike))
                                              Life--is like--

124   You say that (to his
125   fuckin' face).
         [   ]
126 Na?: ((laugh))
127   No: a bowl-- of cherries
128 Ph: An' sometimes he always gotta be
129   ((making a fish mouth)).
                 [   ]
130 Na, others: ((laugh))
                  [   ]
131 Lu: An' sometimes
132   I don't like--I--
         [   ]
133 Ph: He looks like a *fish*. ((grins))
134 Many: ((laugh))
135 Na: Wait* a minute now. Sometimes I don'   *((gestures with hand at these
136   like what's going* on anymore during   points))
137   breaks* 'n' during lunch* , an'
138   leav*ing me alone, by myself, you
139   know, an'--I been through this
140   at least a couple times now before=
141 Ph: ((staring at Lucille))
142   =With Randy Roe.
143   (1.0)
144 Na: ((lower tone)) Well. Either that
145   or I'm (eating) alone.
                   [   ]
146 Ph: 'N--
147   An' another thing makes me mad
148   (about Sandra--) Sandra Castle and Randy
149   Roe *I* don't believe (bof of them)

```
150        are cousins. I do not believe that
151        either. I think Randy Roe make up
152        stories. Bof of them cous--(I don't
153        believe it). Both of them don't
154        have (no) last names.
155        ((to John)) Do you believe that?
156 Jo:   Well...
157        (3.0)
158        I don't. Um.
159 No:   I do.
160 Na:   There's something awful fishy goin'
161        on (                              ).
                [                          ]
162 Ph:      An' (              ) (Lucille).
163        ((pointing to Lucille)) You have
164        a right to sneak your nose in. You
165        have a right to, uh. (Both of them)
166        is not cousins. I believe that.
167        An' I think Randy Roe wants
168        to make up stories because s--he
169        wants to make me in trouble.
170        An' that's what he's
171        tryin' to do: get me
                [                    ]
172 Jo:   Uh, Philly?
173 Ph:   in trouble.
174 Lu:   (           )
                [                    ]
175 Jo:   Sometimes he got--
176        he got me in big trouble, too.
177 Ph:   Keep away from him. For good.
178 Jo:   No, listen.
179 Ph:   An' I don't care
180        if he try to kill me.
                [                    ]
181 Jo:   I know what he did.
182        I know what he did. He almost
183        killed my brother Dennis one
184        time.
185 Ph:   ((smiling))    (            )
186        (           ).
                [                          ]
187 Jo:   He was getting very meany.
188        An' an'--he was (meaning) to, uh,
189        scratch his pants up.
191 Ph:   That's a bad thing.
                [                          ]
192 Jo:   An', an' he blamed it
193        on me, because--it got blamed on
```

194   me, because when I went home that
195   day, my brother Dennis told my mom
196   that Randy Roe uh: scratched his
197   pants up.
198 Ph: Don't let him to do that again, make
199   your mother mad.
200 Jo: And my mom bawled me out.
201   That's all.

Episode L

 1 Jo: I got (one more) to, uh--read Jim,
 2   O.K.?
 3 JT: Make it quick. We're late.
 4 ( ): We're late.
 5 ( ): We're late.
        [   ]
 6 Al?: We're late.
 7 Jo: All right.
        [   ]
 8 ( ): (   )
 9 Al?: I wanna get outside.
10 Jo: Now I'm--
        [   ]
11 ( ): (   )
        [   ]
12 ( ): (   )
13 Jo: Now I'm--   I'm--
        [   ]
14 No: Read it (your Sundays).
15 Jo: I--I am gonna make my own decision
16   about Randy Roe.
17   ( ):   C'mon.
                                              [   ]
18   ( ):   (   ).
19 Jo: I'm not gonna talk to him no more.
20   ( ):   (   )
21 Jo: An' I'm gonna be on Timmy's side.   (   )
22 No: That's ridiculous,
23   (.).
        [   ]
24 Ti: All right, John.   JT et al.: ((Carry
        (Shakes hands with John))
25 Jo: I'm goin' with you, not him.   on muffled
                          [   ]
26 Ph: Hey, Timmy.   side conver-
27 Ti: ((Rips page from diary,   sations))
28   crumples it, throws it away))

III:5. *Wolfgang Wildgen*: Catastrophe Theoretic Semantics: An Elaboration and Application of René Thom's Theory.
Amsterdam, 1982. iv, 124 pp. Paperbound.

III:6. *René Dirven, Louis Goossens, Yvan Putseys and Emma Vorlat*: The Scene of Linguistic Action and its Perspectivization by SPEAK, TALK, SAY and TELL.
Amsterdam, 1982. v, 186 pp. Paperbound.

III:7. *Thomas Ballmer*: Biological Foundations of Linguistic Communication. Towards a Biocybernetics of Language.
Amsterdam, 1982. x, 161 pp. Paperbound.

III:8. *Douglas N. Walton*: Topical Relevance in Argumentation.
Amsterdam, 1982. viii, 81 pp. Paperbound.

IV:1. *Marcelo Dascal*: Pragmatics and the Philosophy of Mind. Vol. I.
Amsterdam, 1983. xii, 207 pp. Paperbound.

IV:2. *Richard Zuber*: Non-declarative Sentences.
Amsterdam, 1983. ix, 123 pp. Paperbound.

IV:3. *Michel Meyer*: Meaning and Reading. A Philosophical Essay on Language and Literature.
Amsterdam, 1983. ix, 176 pp. Paperbound.

IV:4. *Walburga von Raffler-Engel*: The Perception of Nonverbal Behavior in the Career Interview.
Amsterdam, 1983. viii, 148 pp. Paperbound.

IV:5. *Jan Prucha*: Pragmalinguistics: East European Approaches.
Amsterdam, 1983. v, 103 pp. Paperbound.

IV:6. *Alex Huebler*: Understatements and Hedges in English.
Amsterdam, 1983. ix, 192 pp. Paperbound.

IV:7. *Herman Parret*: Semiotics and Pragmatics. An Evaluative Comparison of Conceptual Frameworks.
Amsterdam, 1983. xii, 136 pp. Paperbound.

IV:8. *Jürgen Streeck*: Social Order in Child Communication. A Study in Micro-ethnography.
Amsterdam, 1983. vii, 130 pp. Paperbound.

V:1. *Marlene Dolitsky*: Under the Tumtum Tree: From Nonsense to Sense, a Study in Non-automatic Comprehension.
Amsterdam, 1984. vii, 119 pp. Paperbound.

V:2. *Roger G. van de Velde*: Prolegomena to Inferential Discourse Processing.
Amsterdam, 1984. viii, 100 pp. Paperbound.

V:3. *Teun Van Dijk*: Prejudice in Discourse. An Analysis of Ethnic Prejudice in Cognition and Conversation.
Amsterdam, 1984. x, 170 pp. Paperbound.

V:4. *Henk Haverkate*: Speech Acts, Speakers and Hearers. Reference and Referential Strategies in Spanish.
Amsterdam, 1984. xi, 142 pp. Paperbound.

V:5. *Lauri Carlson*: "Well" in Dialogue Games: A Discourse Analysis of the Interjection "Well" in Idealized Conversation.
Amsterdam, 1984 (publ. 1985). ix, 111 pp. Paperbd.

V:6. *Danilo Marcondes de Souza Filho*: Language and Action: A Reassessment of Speech Act Theory.
Amsterdam, 1984 (publ. 1985). ix, 167 pp. Paperbd.

V:7. *Lars Qvortrup*: The Social Significance of Telematics: An Essay on the Information Society.
Amsterdam, 1984 (publ. 1985). xi, 230 pp. Paperbd.

V:8. *J.C.P. Auer*: Bilingual Conversation.
Amsterdam, 1984 (publ. 1985). ix, 116 pp. Paperbd.

VI:1. *Jean-Pierre Desclés, Zlatka Guentchéva & Sebastian Shaumyan*: Theoretical Aspects of Passivization in the Framework of Applicative Grammar.
Amsterdam, 1985 (publ. 1986). viii, 115 pp. Paperbd.

VI:2. *Jon-K Adams*: Pragmatics and Fiction.
Amsterdam, 1985 (publ. 1986). vi, 77 pp. Paperbd.

VI:3. *Betsy K. Barnes*: The Pragmatics of Left Detachment in Spoken Standard French.
Amsterdam, 1985 (publ. 1986). viii, 123 pp. Paperbd.

VI:4. *Luigia Camaioni, Cláudia de Lemos, et al.*: Questions on Social Explanation: Piagetian Themes reconsidered.
Amsterdam, 1985 (publ. 1986). viii, 141 pp. Paperbd.

VI:5. *Jef Verschueren*: International News Reporting: Metapragmatic Metaphors and the U-2.
Amsterdam, 1985 (publ. 1986). viii, 105 pp. Paperbd.

VI:6. *Sharon Sabsay, Martha Platt, et al.*: Social Setting, Stigma, and Communicative Competence: Explorations of the Conversational Interactions of Retarded Adults.
Amsterdam, 1985 (publ. 1986). v, 137 pp. Paperbd.

VI:7. *Nira Reiss*: Speech Act Taxonomy as a Tool for Ethnographic Description: An Analysis Based on Videotapes of Continuous Behavior in two New York Household.
Amsterdam, 1985 (publ. 1986). ix, 153 pp. Paperbd.

VI:8. *Saleh M. Suleiman*: Jordanian Arabic Between Diglossia and Bilingualism: Linguistic Analysis.
Amsterdam, 1985 (publ. 1986). xvi, 131 pp. Paperbd.